THE YUKON RIVER TRAIL GUIDE

Archie Satterfield

Stackpole Books

THE YUKON RIVER TRAIL GUIDE

Copyright © 1975 by
Archie Satterfield

Published by
STACKPOLE BOOKS
Cameron and Kelker Streets
Harrisburg, Pa. 17105

All rights reserved, including the right to reproduce this book or portions thereof in any form or by any means, electronic or mechanical, including photocopying, recording, or by any information storage and retrieval system, without permission in writing from the publisher. All inquiries should be addressed to Stackpole Books, Cameron and Kelker Streets, Harrisburg, Pennsylvania 17105.

Printed in the U.S.A.

Library of Congress Cataloging in Publication Data

Satterfield, Archie.
  The Yukon River trail guide.

  Bibliography: p.
  1. Yukon Valley—Description and travel—Guide-books. 2. Boats and boating—Alaska—Yukon Valley. 3. Lakes—Alaska—Yukon Valley. I. Title.
F912.Y9S27   917.98'6'045   75-11907
ISBN 0-8117-2053-5

TO
*Cassandra, Erin and Scott,
who went down the river with us,
and to Sarah,
who joined us for the lake trip.*

Contents

Acknowledgments 9

About the Photos 11

About the Maps 13

Introduction 17

1 Some Yukon River Background 19

2 Trip Planning Considerations 30
       Where to Write for Information   31
       Customs Regulations   31
       Fire Permits and Licenses   31
       Kinds of Boats   33

    Miscellaneous Equipment   35
    Time Elements   36
    Weather   36
    Boating Season   37

3 By Lake to Tagish   39

    Lake Bennett to Tagish   40
    Lake Atlin to Tagish   49

4 Tagish to Hootalinqua   66

    Marsh Lake, the Yukon River to Whitehorse   66
    Whitehorse to Hootalinqua   73

5 Hootalinqua to Fort Selkirk   85

    Hootalinqua to Little Salmon   86
    Little Salmon to Carmacks   90
    Carmacks to Fort Selkirk   95

6 Fort Selkirk to Dawson City and Journey's End   116

    Camps, Way Stations and Creeks below Selkirk   118
    Stewart Island   123
    Last Overnight Camp   126
    Dawson City   133

7 Tributary Rivers   150

    Teslin River   152
    Big Salmon River   152
    Pelly River   154
    Macmillan River   155
    White River   156
    Stewart River   156
    Sixtymile River   157

Suggested Reading   158

Acknowledgments

In Whitehorse: Karl Crosby, John Guldner, Ken Sillak, Don Sawatsky, Joy Denton, Brian Speers, Paul Lucier, Alan Innes-Taylor, Dennis Senger, Cal Waddington, G. I. Cameron, the project geologist's staff and several people whose names I did not get but who, nevertheless, helped with my travels up there.

On the river: The Mountie in Carmacks for not attempting to arrest me when my young son asked, loudly, why I had not bought a fishing license (I wasn't fishing, but didn't want to tackle the chore of convincing a Mountie); Danny Roberts and his family at Fort Selkirk, for good company and information; Rudy and Yvonne Burian at Stewart Island for information and a place to buy a candy bar where one would not expect a candy bar;

to Pete and Mary for tea and an insight into the new settlers along the river.

In Dawson City: Dick Stevenson, Roger Mendelsohn, John Gould, the late Mike Comadina, A. Fuhre and Mike Stutter.

In Vancouver, B. C.: Myron Laka, manager of the Yukon House; Marjorie Robertson, formerly of the Yukon House; Brian Martin, one of the best raconteurs to leave the Yukon, and Dennis Bell, formerly of the Canadian Press.

In Washington: *The Seattle Post-Intelligencer* and *The Seattle Times,* for permitting me to go to the Yukon on assignment when they knew I actually was playing; the National Park Service, Pacific Northwest Region; Ralph Munro, assistant to Gov. Dan Evans, who virtually forced me to make one trip down the river.

In Atlin: Joe and Carol Florence for information and fantastic moose steaks; Stefan Shearer for guide services and companionship, the Reg Brooks of Grahame Inlet for instructions and conversation late into the night.

About the Photos

The historical photos are from the Asahel Curtis Collection at the Washington State Historical Society Museum in Tacoma, Washington. Asahel Curtis was the younger brother of Edward S. Curtis, the famous photographer of North American Indians. Asahel went to the Klondike with the big rush in 1897-98 and photographed the entire stampede, from Seattle to Skagway, over Chilkoot and White Passes, then down the Yukon River to the Klondike gold fields.

The author wishes to thank Anna Ibbotson and Frank Green of the historical museum staff for their invaluable help in selecting the photos, and the Photo Shop in Tacoma for the excellent reproduction they obtained from negatives that, in some cases, were in various stages of disintegration.

The modern photos, except otherwise credited, are by the author.

About the Maps

Be forewarned: None of the maps in this book was drawn to scale. The three showing the headwater lake system were copied from GSC (Geological Survey of Canada) maps, 1:250,000 series, or one inch equals four miles. But after reduction to fit the pages, the scale went out the window.

The river maps from Whitehorse to Dawson City were copied from a set drawn for steamboat pilots, and last revised in 1957. Some changes have been made from those based on a new set drawn recently by Bruce Batchelor of Whitehorse.

The maps make no attempt to match the GSC set. Rather, several sections have been exaggerated to include significant details on the bank. If scale maps were used, such as those drawn by Batchelor, there would be many sections of parallel lines on the pages and nothing else.

So the only feature to rely on for distance is the mileage numbers you will find shown in the river on the maps. Those who must have perfection are invited to purchase a set of the GSC maps, which are here listed. However, they do not name the streams or show all the buildings, nor do they show the cutbanks, cliffs, whirlpools and other intimate details offered in this set. Nevertheless, you won't get lost on the river and you can't miss Dawson City unless you're asleep at the paddle.

The channels shown by the arrows are from the 1957 map, and the boater should not rely heavily on them. In a few cases, the channel that existed then is now on dry land, and it is constantly shifting. The old channel lines were placed on the maps for a general guide and historical interest only. To be accurate, one would have to run the river every year and make appropriate corrections, which is impossible.

Following is a list of all Canada National Topographic maps required for the lakes and rivers covered in this book. They are available from either the Canada Map Office, 615 Booth Street, KIA OE9, Ottawa, Ontario, or Staff Geologist, Government of the Yukon Territory, Whitehorse, Y. T.

Lake Atlin, Grahame Inlet, Taku Arm, Lake Bennett, Nares Lake, Tagish Lake, Marsh Lake and Yukon River to Whitehorse:

Atlin	Sheet No. 104 N
Skagway	104 M
Whitehorse	105 D

Yukon River, Whitehorse to Dawson City:

Whitehorse	105 D
Laberge	105 E
Glenlyon	105 L
Carmacks	115 I
Snag	115 J
Stewart River	115 O
Dawson	116 B, C

Teslin River:

Teslin	105 C
Whitehorse	105 D
Laberge	105 E
Glenlyon	105 L
Carmacks	115 I

About the Maps

Big Salmon River:

Quiet Lake	105 F
Laberge	105 E

Pelly River:

Quiet Lake	105 F
Tay River	105 K
Glenlyon	105 L
Carmacks	115 I

Macmillan River:

Tay River	105 K
Lansing	105 N
Mayo	105 M
Glenlyon	105 L

White River:

Snag	115 J, K
Stewart River	115 O, N

Sixtymile River:

Dawson	116 C, B
Stewart River	115 N, O

Stewart River:

Nadaleen	106 C
Lansing	105 N
Mayo	105 M
McQuesten	115 P
Stewart River	115 O

Introduction

During the past few years the Yukon River, after a respite of nearly 20 years, has again become a major transportation corridor through the Yukon Territory. Where the river formerly was the only route through the Yukon from south to north, and was used for commercial as well as pleasure trips, today it is almost entirely a recreational route. But no guide book existed, and the only source of information was a set of maps used by steamboat skippers, which has been adapted and redrawn for this book, and a wild rivers survey, both of which have been given away by the Yukon government by the thousands.

The casual boater making the trip from headwaters to Dawson City had no source of information to take along that would give a sense of the history, natural history and a directory, so to speak, of what he sees along the bank.

River traffic has doubled and trebled and is still increasing each summer. The numbers will continue to grow due to the establishment of the Klondike Gold Rush International Historical Park. The park, when established, will be the first joint park program between the United States and Canada. It will run from Skagway over Chilkoot and White Passes, down the headwater lakes to the Yukon River and on north to Dawson City.

For all practical purposes, the park already is in existence. The U.S. National Park Service has combined forces with the State of Alaska to preserve the artifacts on Chilkoot and White Passes and has provided rangers to aid hikers during the summer months. In Canada, the federal government has budgeted funds to restore the three remaining paddlewheelers and to restore Dawson City to its turn-of-the-century appearance. Other funds are being used to protect the Canadian side of Chilkoot Pass, and some stabilization of structures in ghost towns along the Yukon will be undertaken.

While the Klondike gold rush of 1897-98 was the most dramatic event in Yukon history, its importance to the river has been offset in later years by the steamboat era that ran from the gold rush to the early 1950s. Nearly all signs of human endeavor along the river are related to the steamboat years, and not to the gold rush itself.

There are some river enthusiasts who prefer going beyond Dawson City into Alaska; to Circle City or Eagle or on down to the Tanana near Fairbanks. This book will be of little value to them beyond Dawson City. I have chosen to limit it to that 600-mile stretch of lakes and river because (1) of the Klondike park, (2) because it makes a good two-week trip, which usually is enough for the average boater on vacation and (3) it is easier to leave the river at Dawson City for land transportation or air service.

The book concludes with brief descriptions of the various tributary rivers between Whitehorse and Dawson City.

If another guide is written to the Yukon going beyond Dawson City, someone else will have to write it. I have no interest in getting lost in that maze of islands, sloughs and slack water in the Yukon Flats. I will abide by the edict laid down by a friend who went to the Tanana: "Only masochists and mosquito bait go through the flats."

1

Some Yukon River Background

Ironies, one might say, are like gold: They are where they are found. But for these purposes, we will limit ourselves to only two concerning the Yukon River at the beginning. Others will occur from time to time, like roils and sweepers and up-wellings along the river.

First, the Yukon begins almost within sight of the Pacific Ocean, yet travels more than 2000 miles before it reaches that ocean. As you cross Chilkoot or White Pass from Alaska into Canada above Skagway, a look backward about 15 miles will reveal the waters of Lynn Canal, a straight, narrow ribbon of Pacific Ocean saltwater that ends at Dyea Inlet, the foot of the Chilkoot Trail which leads into the Yukon system.

The other irony is that the Yukon River undoubtedly was the first major North American river discovered and used by man, and the last discovered by the restless white men. This is not surprising considering its course through a rather hostile environment that discouraged merchants and their traveling salesmen of two centuries ago. It is that same environment that today limits its use for recreational purposes to only about one-fourth of the calendar.

Except for a few legends preserved by the Indians, little is known of life along the river before the advent of the record-keeping white men. Our accurate knowledge goes only to the first contact between the disparate cultures and any records coming from that contact must be tempered with tolerance for cultural differences. In spite of our advanced knowledge and reservoirs of information today, we still cannot always exercise tolerance. In the 17th and 18 centuries, it must have been virtually impossible.

Traditionally, the Indians of the North limited themselves to the forests and left the treeless tundra and Arctic Coast to the Eskimos. In the Yukon and Northern British Columbia, the area we're concerned with here, the Indians were broken down roughly into five major tribes: The Tagish in what is now the Whitehorse, Carcross and Tagish area; the Inland Tlingit, as differentiated from the coastal Tlingit in Southeast Alaska; the Tutchone, especially the northern branch, along the middle section of the river, and the Han in the Dawson City area.

Also playing a major role in the Yukon were the Chilkats of Lynn Canal, a branch of the Tlingits. The Chilkats were the middlemen in trading who dealt with the Interior Indians, exchanging fish oil and white men's trade goods with the Interior tribes for furs, horns and other products.

Little is known about them, except that they had an extremely difficult life. Their life could be a constant reminder, by the way, for those people from the southern part of the continent who plan to go north and live off the land. There are stories from the Indians' oral history of widespread famines over the years, deaths by freezing and occasional forays into cannabilism to survive. Living off the land was, and still is, a risky way to live in the Yukon. The cash economy has much to recommend itself if longevity, low infant mortality and general good health are one's goal in life. It is best to say this early in the book because when one goes on a

Some Yukon River Background

leisurely trip down the Yukon River in midsummer when the temperature ranges up to 90 degrees, the sky fills with fluffy clouds and in the rich valleys the flowers grow and the moose and bear are seen on the river bank, then it is easy to think of the Yukon as a land of plenty.

The old-timers there will agree it is the land of plenty: Plenty cold, plenty months of minus degrees below zero; and plenty work to do during the short summer preparing for winter!

No one could have agreed more than the first white men on the Yukon. The first was Robert Campbell, who established Fort Selkirk at the confluence of the Pelly River and the Yukon in 1843, and the Russians who explored the upper river later. The summers and autumns were pleasant enough, but the long, cold winters which confined the men to the tiny, smelly cabins for months on end were another matter. Considering the circumstances, one marvels that the white men, who had the choice, did not leave the employment of fur companies and head south to become farmers or clerks.

But it was fur, then gold, that brought the white men into the Yukon, and it was the latter that finally caused the Yukon to be settled by permanent white residents and to completely alter the landscape and the social customs.

The history of the gold rush will be told rather briefly here because it has been told so often in so many other books that one risks becoming repetitive before the books begins. A bibliography at the end lists the major books on the subject.

There are a number of versions of how the first gold on the Yukon was discovered and by whom. Was it an employe of the Russian American Trading Co., of the Hudson's Bay Co., both of which were more interested in fur than gold? Or was it a minister, as some versions insist? No matter; the gold was discovered on different feeder streams, the word leaked out and a trickle of prospectors began heading north. One must bear in mind that the 19th century America was addicted to gold rushes: Those in Colorado, in California and smaller ones in the Pacific Northwest. Gold rushes were part of the social order, a cultural inheritance.

It took several years for the biggest discovery, in the Klondike, to be made. In the meantime, prospectors worked the Yukon tributaries and found gold at Circle City, at Forty Mile, at Stewart River and dozens of smaller places. There wasn't enough for a big stampede; only enough to keep the prospectors interested and to justify having trading posts operated by men with a gambling spirit themselves. These traders would continue grubstaking serious prospectors, taking their losses with their gains, always believing the next summer, the next stream, the next prospector would hit it.

They hit the big one in 1896, when a white man named George Washington Carmacks and two Indians, Tagish Charlie and Skookum Jim, the latter his brother-in-law, made the great Klondike discovery on August 17 on a stream called Rabbit Creek, but immediately renamed Bonanza Creek.

The town of Forty Mile was abandoned as the miners rushed upstream against the swift current, poling and tracking their boats, to the Klondike River and up it a short distance to the Bonanza and other streams feeding the small river. One of the traders, Joseph LaDue, set up a sawmill where the Klondike empties into the Yukon and established a town named for George M. Dawson, a Canadian geologist and explorer who was sent to the Yukon in 1887.

The Klondike strike was the dream come true for prospectors. During the remainder of that summer and through the winter they took gold out by the pound. When summer returned and the ice cleared from the river, many were ready to return to their homes and families in the United States (most were from that country rather than Canada, where the gold was found). Thus, it was eleven months after the strike before the rest of the world knew of the event.

Two ships docked in San Francisco loaded with miners on July 15, 1897, but it wasn't until the coastal steamer, *Portland,* landed in Seattle after the men had gone down the Yukon by steamboat to St. Michael, Alaska, and caught the *Portland,* that the full impact of the strike was struck home. A newspaper reporter coined the magic words: "A ton of gold." That started the last, great gold rush and took several thousand inexperienced miners to a place none had heard of in a climate with a temperature range of 100 degrees or more.

There were various routes from the United States and southern

Some Yukon River Background

Canada to the Klondike, and many were promoted by greedy townspeople and steamship lines that resulted in deaths, dismemberments and insanity. The stampeders went up through the interior of Canada from Edmonton, Alberta, an impossible route that killed most of those attempting it; the inland route from Ashford, British Columbia, equally hazardous; the Malispina Glacier route from Alaska; the Copper River route from Cook's Inlet; the "rich man's route," from Seattle to St. Michaels and up the Yukon River, which took more than a year; and finally the Chilkoot and White Passes.

The latter two were the shortest, probably the easiest when all alternatives are considered, but certainly no wilderness jaunt as described by the old poet, Joaquim Miller.

Theoretically, these routes were simple. The stampeders took ships from San Francisco, Seattle, Vancouver and Victoria up the Inside Passage to the head of Lynn Canal to Skagway and Dyea. From Skagway, they went over White Pass only 40 miles to Lake Bennett. From Dyea, nine miles from Skagway, they went 26 miles to Lake Lindeman, or 8 miles farther to Lake Bennett.

Once over the passes, they had to do no more walking. The rest was down the chain of lakes and into the Yukon River and north to Dawson City and the Klondike gold fields. Simple?

Not really. First of all, they had to somehow get roughly a ton of gear from tidewater at Skagway and Dyea over the passes to the lakes. The Canadian Mounties posted at the summits of the passes, which is the international boundary, required each person to bring in at least a year's supply of food. Their requirements brought the weight up to 1150 pounds. Add to that the clothing, tools, firearms, etc., that each person would bring, and it roughed out at a ton.

This had to be either carried on the owner's back or a back he hired to carry it. There were packers with strings of horses and mules on White Pass, but the cost was as high as the market would bear. Horses could not operate well in the Chilkoot because it was too rough. So enterprising businessmen built aerial tramways. In the early stages of the gold rush, Chilkat Indians hired out as packers, but they gradually priced themselves out of business.

This was part of the problem. Other facts included wintering over in the mountains with the blizzards that are common, frigid winds, low temperatures, epidemics of spinal miningitis, theft, murder and avalanches.

After they got themselves and their gear to the lakes, they then had to build or buy boats. They had to saw the green spruce and pine and build a craft that would get them through the lakes, down the river, through the rapids at Miles Canyon and below, then on down the river.

During that mad winter of 1897-98, stampeders were strung out along the trail all the way from tidewater over the passes, beside Lake Bennett, Tagish Lake, Marsh Lake and down the river to Lake Laberge and beyond. All were waiting for the ice to clear from the river and lakes, and those below Lake Laberge were the first to get under way in the spring of 1898 since the river ice clears first.

By the second week of June, the scraggly armada began arriv-

A fair-sized town grew up on the south end of Lake Bennett during the gold rush and was served by steamboats until the White Pass & Yukon Route rails were strung beyond Carcross at the north end of the lake.

A few boatbuilders knew their trade, such as these at work before the ice cleared in early June, 1898, from Lake Bennett.

ing in Dawson City, all 7000-odd boats and rafts. But they were presented with a bad joke. In spite of their efforts during the past several months, all the claims worth staking had been taken by prospectors already in the Yukon. For most, the gold rush was an exercise in futility. Many caught the first paddlewheeler back down the Yukon to St. Michaels, Alaska and home. Others stayed to work for wages because they had no more money. The great gold rush became a bittersweet memory.

In the meantime, another enterprise was underway that would give a permanence to the Yukon River as a transportation corridor. A railroad, to be called the White Pass & Yukon Route, was being built under extremely hazardous circumstances over White Pass. The narrow-gauge rails were stretched to Lake Bennett, which took the walking out of the passes for prospectors and animals (which by the way, had died by the thousand), and finally past the treacherous Miles Canyon, Whitehorse and Squaw Rapids to a spot where steamboats from downriver could land.

Thus began the steamboat and railroad era of the Yukon that

After the stampeders failed to strike it rich at Dawson City, they crammed themselves aboard the steamboats headed back down the Yukon to St. Michaels, Alaska, then home, wiser but no richer.

lasted until the early 1950s, when highways were built and air service established. The railroad still exists and probably always will. The steamboats disappeared from the river.

But for more than 50 years, the steamboats were there. More than 200 were built and operated on the river at different times. They hauled passengers, ore, supplies, and you-name-it between Dawson City and Whitehorse. From Whitehorse to the ocean at Skagway, the narrow-gauge trains took over.

While the WP&YR was under construction, a gold strike was made over the Coast Range near Lake Atlin. For a time the railroad was almost without employes as they flocked over to the vast lake for another stab at striking it rich.

There is a romantic story which tells us Fritz Miller and Kenneth McLaren took a wrong turn somewhere on Chilkoot or White Pass and ended up in the Atlin district. Shrugging, they started panning and lo! gold.

Some Yukon River Background 27

Unfortunately, that is not the case. Nor is it true that a dying prospector with a sack of gold and a rough map led to the discovery there. The facts, on the other hand, appear to be that Fritz Miller's brother, George, went over the Juneau Icecap to Lake Atlin in 1896 and found "colors" but spent an equal amount of time hiding from Indians.

Two years later, in January, 1898, Fritz Miller and Ken McLaren went over to check the prospects for themselves and chose an easier but longer route. They went up the White Pass Trail from Skagway, then swung east from Lake Bennett to Tutshi Lake, down the Tutshi River to Tagish Lake, down it to Grahame Inlet, east up it to the Atlin River, along its banks to Lake Atlin, across it by leaky skiff to the east shore and the feeder streams where the gold was supposed to be.

They found gold on Pine Creek, but left with summer for more supplies in Juneau. They turned around and headed back to Atlin with six other prospectors and the rush to Atlin soon began. When word leaked out, the crews working on the White Pass & Yukon Route roadbed began a mass exodus to Atlin, walking off the job with nearly all the railroad's shovels firmly in hand.

Later on, the Atlin mining followed the course of the Klondike gold fields and hand labor by individual miners was replaced by corporate endeavor and huge dredges.

The steamboat era that followed the gold rush at Dawson City and Atlin and lasted 50-odd years figured prominently on the headwater lakes. The railroad took care of the major problem of Miles Canyon and the rapids just below it, so that there were two separate steamboat routes: One for the Yukon River from Whitehorse downstream, and a second for the lake system from Carcross back to the foot of the Coast Range.

After the railroad was completed, the paddlewheelers no longer steamed on Lake Bennett because the railroad ran its entire length. But they ran from Carcross down Windy Arm, down Tagish Lake into Taku Arm, down its length to the delightful Ben-My-Chree (about which more will be said later), up Grahame Inlet to the Atlin River, where a railroad was built.

This railroad was the shortest line in Canada at the time, and certainly one of the shortest—at just over two miles—in the entire world. It was built to transport cargo from the Grahame Inlet sta-

(Anton Vogee Collection)
The steamboat *Scotia* docked at Scotia Bay on Lake Atlin taking on a load of goods and passengers from the two-mile-long railroad. The tiny steam engine, "Dutchess," pushed the cars one direction, then returned in reverse.

tion called Taku up the riverbank to Lake Atlin's Scotia Bay, where other steamboats were waiting. The tiny train engine, named "The Dutchess," ran forward one way, and reverse the other.

"The Dutchess" and the last remaining lake boat, the *Tutshi,* are still in the lake shore at Carcross. In Atlin, the lake steamboat, *Tarahane,* has been beached on Atlin's waterfront and is being restored by the local historical society.

This, then, is the background of the Yukon River in, one hastens to add, an abbreviated form. As this is being written, no good history of the Yukon since the gold rush era exists, and there is not sufficient space in this work to probe deeply into the last 75 years of that part of the world. However, as the book progresses downstream, historical perspectives will be presented so that the boater, or armchair traveler, will have a general idea of the historical importance of different sections of the river and headwater lakes.

2

Trip Planning Considerations

To begin the trip at Lake Bennett, one must ride the WP&YR train from either Skagway or Whitehorse. If coming from the United States, one will go up the Inside Passage from Seattle to Skagway, either by plane or by Alaska State Ferry, then ride the train from Skagway to Bennett.

Those arriving directly in Whitehorse will have a choice of riding the train back to Bennett and beginning there, or simply putting the boat into the river at Whitehorse and skipping the lake system entirely. The choice made will depend partly on the kind of boat and the time allotted for the trip.

Those driving to the Yukon on the Alaska Highway most likely will begin in Whitehorse, too. If you begin at Atlin, arrangements will have to be made with someone in advance for transportation to or from Whitehorse.

Trip Planning Considerations 31

Where to Write for Information

Your best source of information for the entire lake and river system is the Yukon government: Director, Travel and Information, Box 2703, Whitehorse, Yukon Territory, Canada. This department will provide you with information on transportation, canoe and boat rentals, charter buses, lodging, etc.

Other sources include: Board of Trade, Atlin, British Columbia; White Pass & Yukon Route, Public Relations, Whitehorse, Y.T.; Whitehorse Chamber of Commerce; Klondike Visitors Association, Dawson City, Y.T.; Yukon Canoe Rental, 507 Alexander Street, Whitehorse, Y.T.

Customs Regulations

The major customs regulations to remember when entering Canada are that no handguns are permitted in Canada, and you can bring only two days' food per person into the country. You can bring rifles and shotguns into the country with no problem, however, and so far as food is concerned, you'll have no difficulty finding a wide variety of food in Whitehorse. The selection obviously is narrower in the smaller towns, but you will find all the staples in Atlin, Carcross, Tagish and Carmacks. However, the food will be higher in the smaller towns than in Whitehorse due to transportation problems.

One more thing, a small point but one that can be frustrating: You must have Canadian stamps in order to mail letters up there, just as they must have United States stamps down here. But we tend to forget minor details such as stamps on a long trip, so stop at a post office.

Fire Permits and Licenses

Fire permits must be obtained from Royal Canadian Mounted Police offices for trips into the wilderness. There are no particular problems involved in obtaining them, and it is a good opportunity to ask further questions about your route and to register with the Mounties, also required by law. You simply fill out the form and include your destination, route and estimated time of arrival, then

WP&YR train going over White Pass between Skagway and Bennett

Trip Planning Considerations 33

remember to tell the Mounties when you arrive so no searches will be launched.

Fishing licenses are available at most stores along the routes, and if you're on Lake Atlin, remember that you must have both British Columbia and Yukon licenses if you are traveling north on the lakes into the river. Since most of the Lake Bennett-to-Dawson City route is in the Yukon (except for the first portion of the Lake Bennett trip), Yukon fishing licenses only are required. This is assuming, of course, that you won't be fishing in Lake Bennett.

If you take your own boat for the trip, have proof of ownership of it and other expensive items. You may be asked to register your equipment with customs, such as cameras, firearms, boats and other gear.

You must also remember that all artifacts in Canada are protected by federal law. This includes old bottles you might dig at a garbage dump, telegraph insulators found along the river, even broken dishes and rusty buckets found at old woodcutters' camps.

If you buy anything remotely like an artifact—an antique for example—be sure you are given a receipt and save it for clearing customs when leaving the country.

Kinds of Boats

The reader must assume each guidebook author has his own set of prejudices, limitations of intelligence, and most of all, a dearth of experience in some matters, including the very subjective subject of boats.

The author has traveled on the lakes and river in inflatable boats (Zodiac and Avon), freighter canoes and the flat-bottomed river boats. He has not traveled in paddle-powered craft, such as kayaks and canoes, and he isn't certain he wants to for the simple reason he likes stability beneath his big feet. However, there are those who prefer the latter, and there are even some river travelers who use an amphibious automobile, which is a bit much. Homemade log rafts are only a little better, although some use them with success and enjoy themselves tremendously.

With these limitations and prejudices in mind, following is a general rating of craft based on the author's personal experience and that of others he's talked to:

KAYAKS—Many people use them on the lakes and river, but they have obvious disadvantages. They are dangerous in heavy weather on the lakes, they are difficult to get into and out of, they do not carry much equipment, and what they do carry is usually beyond easy reach when needed. They are more practical on the river than lakes, and remember—you will be going across Lake Laberge, noted for its sudden and vicious squalls. There is virtually no whitewater on the trip to require the maneuverability advantages.

CANOES—These, too, are dangerous on the big lakes and are easy to swamp or flip in the heavy swells. However, on the river, they are great: silent, easy to paddle and cheaper to rent or transport. But bear in mind that the river and lake drownings during the past few years have been from canoes.

INFLATABLE BOATS—These are about evenly divided between pluses and minuses. They are virtually impossible to sink (in the case of the expensive models such as Zodiac and Avon) because they have so many flotation chambers. They are easy to transport to the North and very comfortable for sitting because any surface is a potential seat. They are equally good on the lakes and the river.

The minuses include their tendency to develop leaks ranging from pinpricks to gaping holes, and over to the bank you go for repairs. They have a tendency (with a 20-hp motor) to plow through the water, especially when attempting to run upstream, and their fuel consumption can be greater than a freighter canoe or river boat due to the drag.

FREIGHTER CANOES—These remarkable boats are the most stable, biggest and easiest of all to handle. The modified V-bottoms are the best for both lake and river, and they are incredibly tough and seaworthy; you could register a 22-footer in

Trip Planning Considerations

Liberia or Panama and go into the shipping business with them. Six or seven people and gear can easily fit into a 20 or 22-footer powered by a 20-hp motor, and they draw so little water that going aground in the river is no great problem. The author ranks these tops for both lake and river.

RIVER BOATS—These flat-bottomed boats are a close second and would be first were it not for the inherent problems with a flat bottom. On the lakes they have a tendency to plow through, or under, the waves to drench you and they bounce and bob and plop across the heavy swells. They are the best on the river. They offer more room than the freighters, haul more people per foot than a freighter and are the least likely of all powered boats to run aground. These are strongly recommended for a large party of congenial people. As with the freighters and canoes, they can be rented in Whitehorse, and for a group of six or eight preferring a powered boat, the cost would be minimal spread over the whole party.

As stated before, all types of boats have navigated the river and lakes in safety, but those traveling on the lakes in kayaks or canoes must be prepared for some tense moments. If the wind doesn't blow, they can return and accuse the author of cowardice. But for those who get swamped or worse, I'll say it now and never again: You were warned!

Miscellaneous Equipment

There is no use making up a list of recommended equipment here because it is not like a backpacking trip in which everything will be carried on your back for two weeks. Instead, consider this a *reminder* list:

Repair kits for canoes, motors, tents, rubber boots, stoves, etc; first aid kit (no snakebite kit since there are no snakes in the Yukon); tent with waterproof fly and insect netting; mosquito repellent (at least twice what you think you'll need, or two small bottles per person); mosquito coils, which are small smudge-pot gadgets that drive the varmints from cabins you might use along the way; a tarp to cover your gear in the boat and the boat itself at night in case of rain; strong waterproof bags for your delicates, such as sleeping bag and food and cameras (surplus ammunition cans are popular for this); sunglasses with elastic keeper band; sunburn lotion; rain suit; waterproof gloves; woolen clothing (you are going to get wet—assume that and dress accordingly); extra nylon rope; hat; knife and whetstone; collapsible water jug and water purification tablets.

The fewer breakable items you bring the better. If possible, do not take a standard packframe since the frame will bend easily. A day pack or summit-type pack without an exterior frame is best.

It is so obvious that it should not need saying, but you *must* have a good life jacket for each person in the boat, and they *must* be worn, with the zipper zipped or the ties tied, at all times. To refuse to wear them is to court disaster.

Time Elements

Following is only a rough estimation of the time involved in the various legs of the journey. The trips can be made faster or slower, depending on one's desires and time. However, these times allow for bad weather, frequent stops to poke around the shores and generally enjoy oneself. The lake times are with powered boats; allow at least two more days if paddling.

    Bennett to Whitehorse — 3 days
    Whitehorse to Dawson — 10 days
    Atlin to Whitehorse (direct route with no side trips) — 4 days
    Atlin to Whitehorse (all stops) — 10 days

Weather

The usual image of a Yukoner is a cross between Yosemite Sam and Santa Claus with icy beard and stoplight nose. Above him is a comic-strip balloon saying "Forty below and blowing," or something like that.

Don't you believe it. It certainly gets that cold in the winter, but you will be traveling in the summer when the days are long (24 hours of light in June), and you most likely will have temperatures up to the 80s or even higher.

There is little rainfall in the Yukon interior, through which the

Trip Planning Considerations

river flows, and the annual average is about 12 inches. However, you can expect showers and should be prepared.

There are exceptions, of course. For example, the summers of 1973 and 1974 were extremely wet and colder than usual. Some nights in August were below freezing, and rainy, overcast weather was common. Again, you must be prepared with warm clothing, raingear and waterproof tent fly.

Boating Season

As a general rule, the boating season runs from mid-June until the end of September. The only "if" in June is if the ice has cleared from the lakes. Most years the ice is gone by June 10, but there are exceptions when the ice stays in the lakes until the third week of June. In this case, you will have to bypass the lakes and begin the trip at Whitehorse, since Lake Laberge usually clears ahead of the upper lakes because of the river at each end.

The river is usually high in June and slowly diminishes as the summer progresses. During the high-water period, the major problem is avoiding all the debris in the water—stumps, whole

Interior of WP&YR chair car

trees, garbage picked up on the river banks, etc. The river is faster at high-water periods with a flow up to nine to ten miles per hour in places. By mid-summer, this drops to five to seven miles per hour in the portion of the river we are concerned with here.

By early September, the river is quite low and the risk of running aground increases. Also, the weather is more unpredictable and certainly colder. It is best to plan trips from mid-June through late August.

3

By Lake to Tagish

Lake Bennett was the end of the Chilkoot and White Pass Trails during the gold rush, and today is a lunch-stop for passengers on the WP&YR. Trains from both Skagway and Whitehorse meet at Bennett during the noon hour, have lunch (part of your ticket price and all you can eat), then continue on. The train crews are changed here; Canadian crews run between Whitehorse and Bennett, American crews back and forth between Skagway and Bennett.

When you arrive on the train, you first should retrieve all your gear from the baggage car before having lunch to be sure you aren't left standing alone on the roadbed watching your gear depart without you.

Only a few traces of the gold rush and railroad construction stage remain around Bennett. The most prominent relic is the old church on the hill looking down the lake. It was begun in 1899, when several hundred men were still at Bennett, some working on the railroad, others either getting ready to head down the river to the Klondike or working in the shipyards at Bennett building vessels ranging from paddlewheelers to skiffs and rafts.

When the railroad was completed the boatyards disappeared virtually overnight, and the church was left unfinished. The exterior was completed, but there are no walls, no floors and an uncompleted ceiling inside. The railroad and government have kept the church from gracefully falling in on itself, and funds are being allocated by the Canadian federal government to preserve it.

Clustered around the church are some cabins and shacks used by trappers or migrant squatters laying over in Bennett on their way elsewhere. Those that are in decent shape are usually occupied; the others offer little more shelter than a spruce tree.

On the hilltop behind the church is a cemetery dating back to the gold rush era, and a footpath leads up the stream that connects Lake Bennett and Lake Lindeman. However, it peters out when the going gets rough. The Chilkoot Trail follows the high ground over the rocks between the railroad and the stream, and winds back through the thin timber to Lake Lindeman and up the chain of lakes to the summit.

Just below the church on the lake shore is a group of pilings built during the brief steamboat era on the lake, and against the steep bank directly beneath the church is a series of cavities dug out of the sand bank. These depressions date back to the gold rush when the stampeders leveled out sites against the hillside for tents and cabins.

Lake Bennett to Tagish

Most boaters cast off as close to the railroad depot as possible for obvious reasons: It is closest. Since it is unlikely you will be camping on this part of Lake Bennett, you had just as well get the boats to the water the fastest way and get away from civilization as soon as possible.

Church at Lake Bennett

Lake Bennett (named by Lt. Schwatka during his trip up there in 1883 for James Gordon Bennett, the publisher of the *New York Herald Tribune* who sponsored the Stanley search in Darkest Africa for Dr. Livingston; I wouldn't presume to guess why Schwatka named it for him though) is some 26 miles long with steep mountains jutting up from either side at the southern end. The Bennett Range rises on the west side and a series of peaks on the east side crowned by Montana Mountain, 7280 feet, about halfway down the lake.

The southern section of the lake is never more than a mile wide and usually less than a half mile wide, and has all the classic characteristics of a fjord. Camp sites are sparce along this section, except on the east side between the WP&YR tracks and the lake. It need not be said that camping beside a railroad track leaves much to be desired.

The best campsites are found on the small, low islands that form the boundary between British Columbia and the Yukon. Farther north, beyond the entrance of West Arm, are some campsites on the west side. But you must use caution crossing the lake near the West Arm entrance due to the strong winds that frequently whip down from the Coast Range.

The scenery along the lake is spectacular with sheer cliffs jutting upward from the water's edge and numerous waterfalls streaming down from melting snowfields above. The lake water is tinted green and the bottom is visible to forty feet below. The wilderness experience is marred only by the presence of the railroad tracks, but some boaters traveling through the sparsely populated North find the tracks and trains reassuring while becoming accustomed to vast open spaces and deep silences.

Perhaps the most spectacular scene on Lake Bennett is when one crosses the open end of West Arm and the row of high, snow-covered peaks of the Coast Range come into view. It gives the lake a sudden, arctic look quite different from the lower, barren peaks closer to the lake.

Lake Bennett ends at the small community of Carcross, where a very short stream empties Lake Bennett into a small lake named Nares, which in turn feeds into Tagish Lake.

Carcross originally was called Caribou Crossing because the woodland caribou (as differentiated from the migratory caribou

By Lake to Tagish 43

of the Arctic Coast) used the shallow stream as a crossing (no surprise in this town's name, is there?). Credited with naming the town is Bishop William Carpenter Bompas, the famous Anglican priest who lived in the Yukon for years before and during the gold rush. It appears that the bishop was fond of abbreviating whenever possible to save himself from writer's cramp, and thus was Carcross born for cartographers.

Carcross has a post office, a hotel with bar and restaurant, a general store, service station and railroad depot. Across the railroad bridge, on the south side of Nares Lake, is the Indian community and cemetery where Skookum Jim, Tagish Charlie and Kate Carmacks, George W. Carmack's first wife, were buried.

The most prominent landmarks in Carcross are the steamboat *Tutshi* and the little railroad engine, "The Dutchess." As mentioned earlier, the *Tutshi* ran from Carcross down Tagish Lake, Taku Arm and Grahame Inlet to the railroad depot at Taku, where "The Dutchess" took over and pulled the cargo and passengers up to Lake Atlin. The *Tutshi* is being restored by the federal and territorial government and is one of only three paddlewheelers left along the river.

Lake Bennett on a calm day

CHILKOOT TRAIL

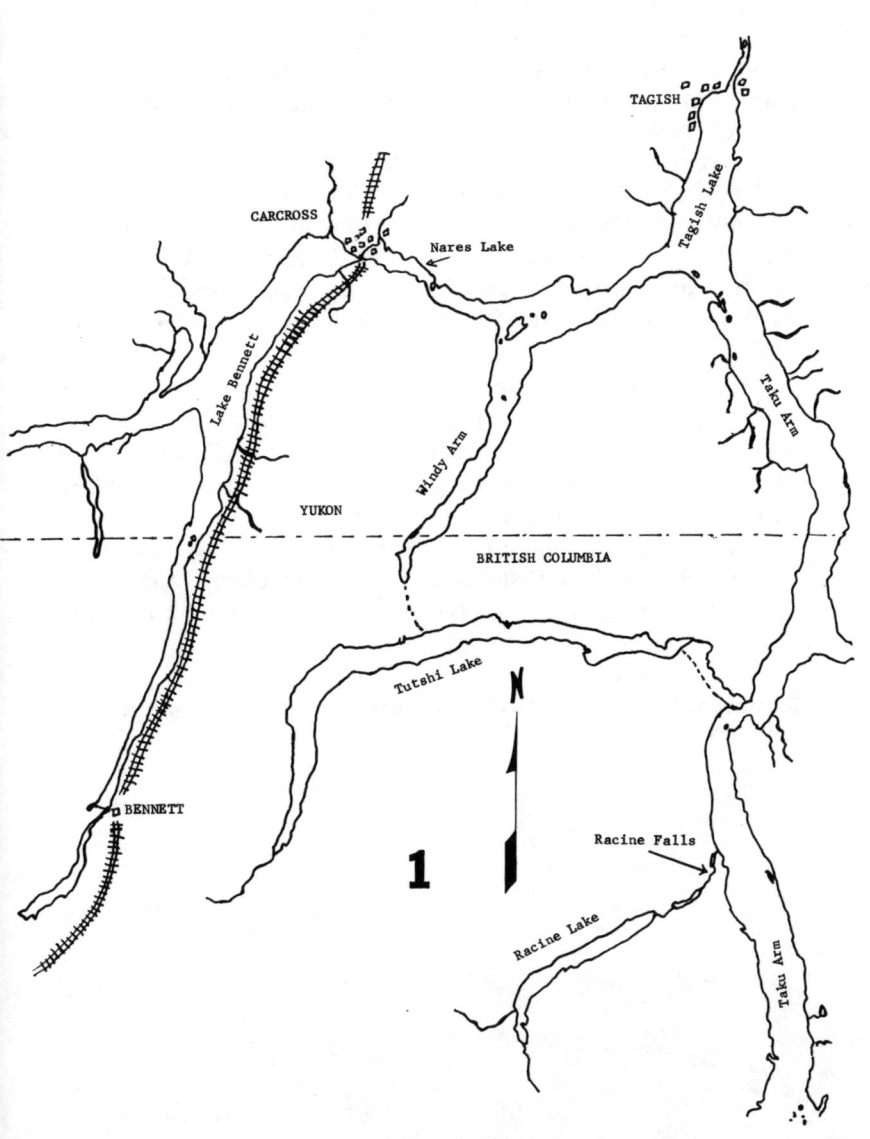

There are good campsites near Carcross, the best of which is on the low sand dunes along the shore west of town. However, it is best to camp in the bush due to the incidence of theft in towns (ah, sweet civilization). Other excellent campsites are found down Nares Lake and on the shore of Tagish Lake, only a short paddle from Carcross.

While in Carcross it is best you check your larder for food and fill up your tanks with fuel. You will be a day or two, depending on the weather, from the next grocery store and petrol station at Tagish. However, you might want to take side trips down Windy Arm or Taku Arm. It is best to always have a week's supply of food with you and always top off your fuel tanks when you have a chance.

All these items are available in Carcross, plus one delicious treat that will test your strength of character in rationing out goodies. That is the cookies manufactured in Canada called "Digestive Biscuits." Don't let the medicinal title confuse you. They are scrumptious.

Nares Lake runs three miles between Bennett and Tagish, a shallow, narrow lake that more closely resembles a broad, slow river. It is picturesque with Nares Mountain rising on its north

Steamboat *Tutshi* with WP&YR steam engine, "*Dutchess*," and stage at Carcross

Rear view of *Tutshi* with new paddlewheels installed

side and Montana Mountain on the south. The shore is wooded with willow, spruce and poplar and has several open grassy areas. Most of the best camping sites are on the south shore. On a windy day, Nares usually is very calm and offers a brief respite from fighting the swells of the larger lakes it connects.

Tagish Lake runs about 17 miles from Nares to the broad stream that connects it to Marsh Lake. About three miles down the lake on the southern side is Windy Arm, a fjord that cuts back into the mountains to terminate beneath Mt. Racine and Mt. Conrad.

It is best to follow the north shore of Tagish Lake across the entrance of Windy Arm in case of strong winds and wave action. The best camping sites are along the north shore, which has a series of low, terraced flats with small streams emptying into the lake.

After passing Windy Arm, the scenery opens up considerably and the surrounding mountains take on a gray color. Some boaters recommend crossing the lake to the south shore beyond Windy Arm to take what protection the shore has to offer from the prevailing south winds. Then, just before the entrance of Taku Arm, cross back again to the north shore so the south wind will be almost directly from the stern. Obviously, the boater will have to decide for himself which is best for his purposes. Usually—not always, of course—one can see the whitecaps of Windy Arm and Taku Arm a mile or two away, which will give adequate time to switch sides of the lake.

Those wishing to explore Windy Arm will be treated to a lake similar in appearance to Bennett sans railroad, with steep mountains rising from near the lake shore. It is 12 miles long and limited of camp sites.

About four miles down the lake on the west side is the abandoned town of Conrad, which had hotels, stores, restaurants and churches during the first decade of this century. It was the headquarters of Conrad Consolidated, Ltd., which operated a mine nearby until 1912 when the mine and town were abandoned. A few old buildings including the mine itself remain along with relics of the period.

At the end of Windy Arm is a three-mile-long portage trail that leads over to Tutshi Lake, a long, narrow and curving lake some 200 feet higher than the larger lakes around it.

At the risk of being repetitious, you should allow extra time while traveling the lakes to sit out rough weather. More lives have been lost on Tagish Lake where Windy Arm enters than any other place along the lakes or Yukon River.

As you follow the curve of Tagish Lake around to the north from the entrance of Taku Arm, civilization returns in the form of summer homes built mostly by Whitehorse residents on the north shore. Most are clustered along the broad, shallow stream connecting Tagish and Marsh Lake.

Toward the head of Tagish Lake, the water becomes shallow and power boaters should throttle back, watch for the bottom and stay in the middle of the stream. The river moves at about two miles per hour and offers excellent lake trout fishing.

The small town of Tagish is near the end of the stream just before it enters Marsh Lake. A spur of the Alaska Highway, which runs from Jake's Corner to Carcross and up to Whitehorse, crosses the stream at Tagish and usually there are so many people fishing on the bridge that you have to be careful to avoid getting entangled in a line.

By Lake to Tagish

Tagish is the site of the first permanent establishment of the Mounties, who set up a post there to collect customs and serve as a checkpoint for stampeders enroute to the Klondike. Before that, the Tagish band of Indians had camps there because of the good fishing and hunting nearby.

Today, there is a territorial park on the east side just upstream from the bridge, grocery stores and service stations, a Mountie post and numerous permanent and summer homes. On the east side of the bridge is Tagish Annie's, a popular bakery where you can buy freshly baked bread, pies and other pastries. On the west side of the bridge and down the road about 100 yards is a grocery store with a good selection of staples, plus gifts and other tourist items.

Camping at Tagish is limited to the unimproved territorial park, but good campsites can be found on Marsh Lake.

Lake Atlin to Tagish

There are many who believe Lake Atlin and the small town of Atlin is the most beautiful area in the North, an opinion difficult to fault. The lake is the largest natural lake in British Columbia and is 66 miles long and from two to five miles wide. It is studded with islands ranging from tiny rocks to the vast Teresa Island with 6755-foot Birch Mountain. The view across the lake from the town of Atlin is one of the most impressive anywhere in the world. Atlin Mountain (6656 feet) rises majestically from the lake and one never tires of watching the play of sunlight on its summit and ridges. A rock glacier flows slowly, steadily from a cirque high up on its face, and the view across to it is accented with the small islands between.

The town of Atlin has an easy-going charm, which is being preserved by the new people moving there—many immigrating from the United States—who want to keep the casual life of semi-isolation. Atlin is 61 miles south from the Alaska Highway over a gravel road, and a total of 113 miles from Whitehorse. Since the road ends at Atlin, it is not one of those places travelers see on their way somewhere else; they must be headed for Atlin if they are going to see it.

The visitor to the town should plan on extra time to drive out to

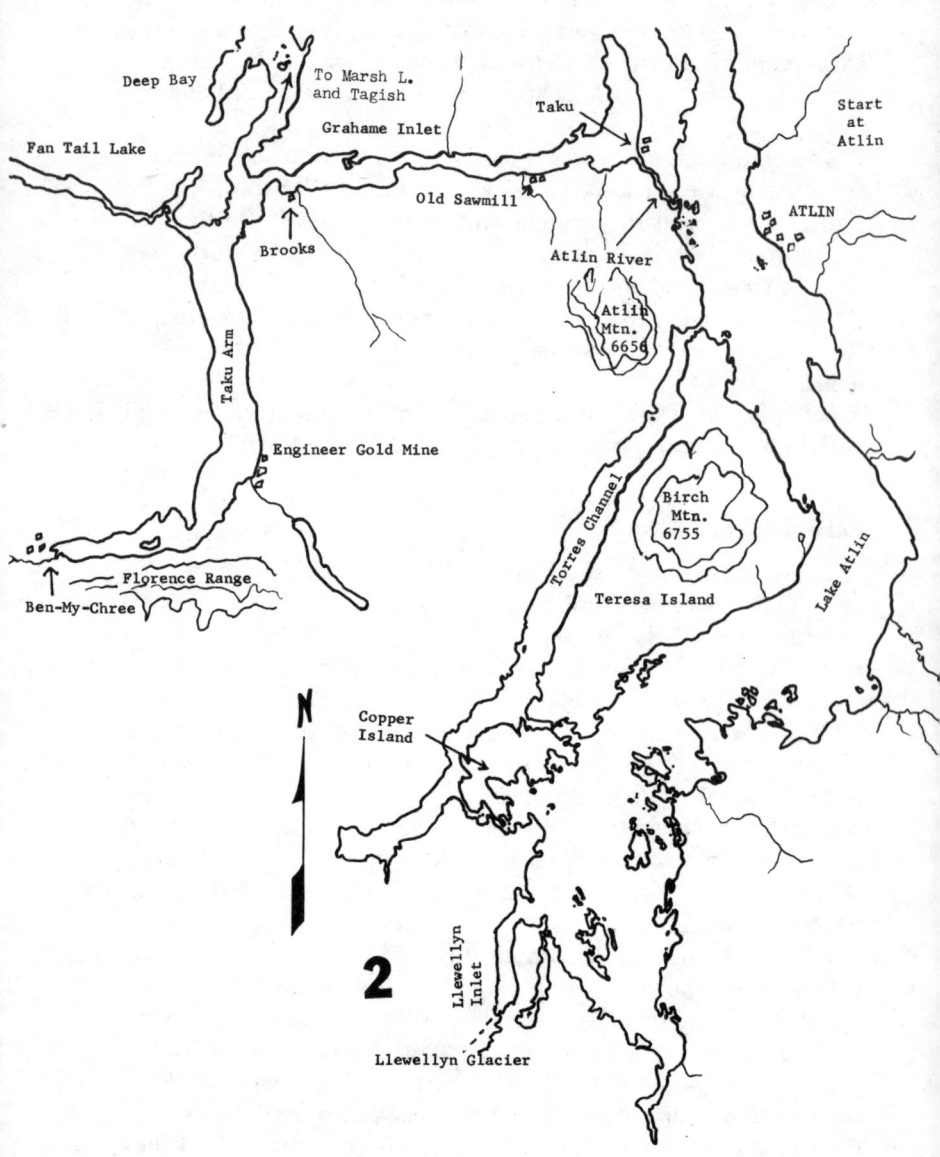

By Lake to Tagish

the ghost town of Surprise at the head of Surprise Lake east of town a few miles. Old gold mining operations and abandoned dredges are scattered along Pine Creek, and a few miners still work and rework the old claims.

An ideal way to see the chain of lakes from Atlin (Lake Atlin, Grahame Inlet, Taku Arm and out to Tagish and Marsh to intersect with the route just described) is to rent a freighter canoe in Whitehorse and arrange for transportation to Atlin, then follow this route to Whitehorse. This makes an excellent trip for a two-week vacation.

The shore of Lake Atlin is virtually deserted today, and only a handful of trappers' cabins can be seen along the route. After you leave sight of the town, it is unlikely another boat will be seen, unless it is the jet boat Joe Florence of Atlin uses to take people up and down the lake on sightseeing trips.

For the boater planning to see the highlights of Lake Atlin, then head for the other lakes, this itinerary is recommended:

Cross the lake from Atlin and follow Torres Channel between the west shore and Teresa Island. The open lake can become very rough and the western shore is acknowledged as the most beautiful. This route takes you past the foot of Atlin Mountain and down a deep channel with protection from the wind.

The best campsites are found at the southern end of Teresa Island and on the small islands south of it, such as Copper Island. There are numerous bays and inlets that can confuse you while seeking a passage through to the open lake, and it is best to ask for landmarks from townspeople before leaving.

Early in the summer you can see cow moose and calves on the islands, where the cows take them for protection from predators.

There are innumerable campsites along the islands and the lake water is clear, cold and pure. Don't hesitate to dip into it for drinking water. The only problem with choosing a campsite is selecting the best of so many choices. However, the most protected campsites appear to be on the northern side of Copper Island in what is known locally as First Passage (the first route from the north between the islands back to the open lake). Second Passage is a wider body of water and more exposed to wind on the shore.

The following day, if the weather is calm, you can go on down the lake to Llewellyn Inlet and hike back to the glacier. Since there are several unpredictable factors involved in traveling on such a large body of water, it's best to break camp and carry everything with you rather than leaving your gear at the first night's camp. You might be raided by a curious, hungry bear; you could become marooned by a storm; you might want to stay at Llewellyn longer and camp there, and worst of all (it has happened) you might forget your landmarks and spend hours looking for your portable home.

Llewellyn Inlet curves around a point, then heads straight back to the Coast Range and Juneau Icecap between sheer cliffs on either side. The trail to the glacier begins at a gravel beach to the west of Llewellyn River, and the trailhead is very protected from the wind.

The trail is named the Stewart James Trail in honor of the late Mr. James who led people back to Llewellyn Glacier. The trail heads up through the gnarled and wind-twisted timber, over boulders and finally down to the moraine plain where the glacier has receded. By crossing the stream at a shallow spot, you can walk all the way to the glacier's snout, which stretches for more than a mile across the valley floor.

An alternate, shorter route follows the stream on the west side to an outcropping of rocks that gives a high, overall view of the glacier and mountains behind. Right at your feet is a clear stream emptying into the glacier milk river that creates a green ribbon in the white river.

The trailhead is an excellent place to camp in case of heavy winds that can sweep down from the icecap in the afternoon and evening. Generally, the early mornings are calm and you can get out of the inlet and back into the protection of the islands before the heavy winds return. It is worth noting here that the deepest spot measured in Lake Atlin is 800 feet, at the head of Llewellyn Inlet.

Local boaters strongly recommend staying with the west shore, but the choice is obviously the individual boater's. If it bothers you to retrace a route, remember that you see things from a different perspective when doing so. Also, the west side of the lake is the most spectacular.

After returning to Atlin, you should reprovision and top off

Post Office with distinctive clock at Atlin, B.C.

Lake steamboat *Tarahne* with Mt. Atlin across Lake Atlin

fuel tanks because it is the last chance until Tagish, which is more than 80 miles by a direct route and about 120 miles if you make all the recommended side trips.

Also recommended is the hiring of a guide in Atlin to help you down the Atlin River. The two-mile-long river runs at about 10 miles an hour and is filled with rapids, boulders, backwashes and shallows. It is very dangerous for canoes and kayaks, less so for larger boats. It should be run in late June or early July before the highwater period in late summer, when the force of the current literally stands the river on its edge in a few places.

Guides are available in Atlin for the trip (one charged $20 in 1973), and worth the investment. The whitewater enthusiast with experience will find the river a source of excitement, if not thrills.

The river begins at Scotia Bay, across the lake to the northwest from Atlin. There are remains of a railroad depot and rail-less ties leading back into the timber. Just below the head of the river are some old, rickety platforms out over the river used by sports fishermen when the railroad was in operation.

Atlin River is difficult to scout from the bank because the railroad bed does not follow closely to the bank. It involves a great deal of brush beating to study the stream before taking it on. When the water is lower in the early summer, the main danger is hitting rocks just below the surface and losing a shear-pin or propeller. To run it without first scouting it involves considerable guesswork because of its shallowness and the inability to quickly maneuver a power boat.

About the only method of scouting it first is to arrange to ride down it with Joe Florence in his jet boat when he is making a run down to Grahame Inlet or beyond. However, Florence runs it at a high speed to stay off the bottom, and you have to be quick of eye.

Obviously, many boats and canoes have run the river with absolute safety, and this is not intended to scare everyone away from it. But it is meant to encourage caution. There have been drownings on the river, some by experienced whitewater kayakers and canoeists.

When the river empties into Grahame Inlet, the safest route is to run on out into the inlet a few hundred feet to avoid the shallow bottom, then swing back around to the railroad station at Taku, where there are sheltered places to tie up out of the wind.

Taku is privately-owned now, but the owner generously permits camping with the plea to leave the area clean. It is an in-

Lake Atlin from freighter canoe on a cool, calm day

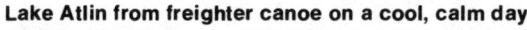

teresting place to camp and poke around the old buildings and railroad shops. The waiting room still has the benches for passengers' convenience and there are numerous tools and pieces of railroad equipment scattered around. The dock is sagging, but still has three narrow-gauge flatcars parked there that were too heavy or expensive to transport out when the steamboats stopped running. Offshore a few feet is the hulk of a steamboat resting on the shallow bottom, and back up in the brush are several small cabins in which railroad workers lived. Some still have furniture in them, but vandals have done their duty and torn much of the furniture into debris.

There is excellent grayling fishing at the river mouth and Grahame Inlet is noted for its lake trout fishing. You can easily spend an extra day at Taku hiking along the lake shore or up the old railroad right-of-way, fishing and trying to imagine the area thirty years ago.

Two miles down the inlet from Taku is an abandoned sawmill with a group of cabins and machine sheds in good condition. A hunting guide uses the cabins in the autumn, which probably accounts for their good condition. Outside are numerous saw

Llewellyn Glacier from trail that leads from Lake Atlin to the glacier

Old steamboat landing and railroad station at Scotia Bay on Lake Atlin at the head of Atlin River.

blades, a steam plant, belts, etc., and several piles of rough-sawn lumber left unsold or undelivered when the sawmill closed. It was built in part to cut ties for the Taku-to-Scotia Bay railroad, but also provided lumber for home building and other uses in the area.

Grahame Inlet runs 16 miles from Taku to Golden Gate, where it enters Taku Arm. A few homes have been built along its shores, mostly summer residences, with the exception of the Reg Brooks home a mile east of the mouth of the Inlet on the south side.

The Brooks and their son, Jim, are the only permanent residents in the area and seldom go to town. They own a cluster of charming log cabins which they rent for $10 a day during the summer. Reg works as a fishing guide in the summer months and the entire family runs traplines during the winter.

An overnight stop at the Brooks is a valuable investment because they are so knowledgable and articulate on wilderness living. Their son was educated by correspondence courses and his knowledge of geology rivals that of a masters' degree candidate.

The Brooks are a reservoir of knowledge on the north and a

visit with them is comparable to a seminar on the subject. Since they live in a remote area, mail service is erratic and they recommend writing at least two months in advance for cabin reservations. Their address is Reg Brooks, General Delivery, Carcross, Yukon Territory, Canada.

Just west of the Brooks home is Golden Gate, the entrance to Taku Arm. The entrance received its name for the brilliant fall colors in the area and the marvelous view of the mountains that opens up as one enters Taku Arm.

Like the other long, narrow lakes of this area, Taku Arm is noted for its heavy swells. Brooks' advice is for boaters to head directly across the arm from Golden Gate, then follow the west shore to the south. Then, when the arm swings sharply to the west toward Ben-My-Chree, cut across to the opposite or south side, and follow that shore on to the end. The return trip with a following sea can be made on the eastern shore to see both sides of the arm and the old mine and town over there.

Taku Arm offers very few campsites along either shore because it is rocky and hemmed in by steep mountains on both sides. By following the shoreline closely, an occasional smooth beach can be found among the rocks.

Florence Range on Taku Arm

By Lake to Tagish

Due to the unpredictable weather, many boaters do not explore the southern half of Taku Arm, below Golden Gate. But the trip is worth whatever discomfort may result. When you reach the final curve in the arm and the Florence Range stands up directly above the icy water, sheer as a canyon wall to more than 7000 feet, the spectacular view is one that is not duplicated anywhere else in the area.

If you cannot continue on to the end of the arm, a small, rocky island near the south shore has good campsites sheltered from the wind and with good beaches for tying up the boat away from the waves. Here, you can pitch a tent with a view out to the stunning Florence Range and watch the midnight sun manipulate the colors of the rock walls and the snow on top.

At the very tip of the arm is a long, rickety pier sticking out over the mudflats from the glacial silt. This is the entrance to the charming ghost town of Ben-My-Chree. To avoid having to play steeplejack and climb up to the dock, it is best to follow the shallow stream on the right, or north, up beside the cliff and beach the boat beneath the pier.

Ben-My-Chree began its colorful history as a mine up in the hills above the buildings. Unfortunately, the mine collapsed and the owners never reopened it. Instead, they began importing plants and trees from all over the world and turned the place into a garden. The owners, Mr. and Mrs. Otto Partridge, came from the Isle of Man and named the place, which in Manx (the Isle of Man language) means "girl of my heart."

Previously, he had operated a sawmill on Lake Bennett, then was associated with a group that ran small sternwheelers on the lakes under the corporate name of Bennett Lake & Klondike Navigation Co.

After Ben-My-Chree became a garden spot in a hostile climate, the steamboats that ran from Carcross to Taku began stopping there on a regular basis. Passengers tramped down the long pier and onto solid ground through a trail that led between pine, fir and numerous kinds of shrubs. They were served tea and cakes and rhubarb wine, and were free to stroll out among the formal gardens and sit in a gazebo with a small, cold stream running through it.

After their deaths six months apart in 1930 and 1931, the

transportation company, WP&YR, continued operating the garden spot until 1955, when the *Tutshi* was beached forever at Carcross.

Ben-My-Chree now is owned by a Vancouver, B.C., resident who hopes to restore it to its original beauty through a foundation.

Due to its isolated location, Ben-My-Chree has not suffered the ravages of vandalism to the extent of other stops along this route. The buildings are still in relatively good shape, the furnishings are intact, and in one building is a bulletin board with several hundred business cards thumbtacked there over the years by visitors.

Part of the pier has sagged down to the mudflat, but the whimsical statuary still stand in the yard, including a gigantic wooden mosquito and a dwarf prehistoric monster.

The next stop of interest on the return trip is at the Engineer gold mine on the east shore about 10 miles from Golden Gate. It is one of those heartbreaking stories among mining circles of a site that had the gold, but never quite enough. It received its name from the fact that a group of engineers working for WP&YR dis-

Engineer Gold Mine on Taku Arm

Dock across mudflats at Ben-My-Chree

covered it and began operating it in 1899. It was sold in 1907, then idled by litigation, then opened again in 1924.

In 1930, a power dam was built on the Wann River, a few miles south of the mine, barely in time for the mine owners to run out of operating capital and close it again. The mine has not been in operation since, but there are always rumors that this or that group is going to open it again.

A trail leads from the mine back down the lakeshore to the power dam, now gone, and a cluster of buildings still stand. Some are owned by summer residents. The mine building runs up the hillside and shows evidence of numerous additions as the mine was enlarged. Most of the machinery is still inside, and there are a number of old, rotting ore sacks lying about with EGM stenciled on them.

As Taku Arm runs past Golden Gate, it narrows somewhat and several islands of various sizes are scattered around. Campsites are abundant north of Golden Gate, and most boaters select one near a stream entering the lake because it is easier to catch grayling at a stream's entrance. The west shore is steeper and less marshy than the east side. It is recommended that you stay on the west side because there will be fewer mosquitos than in the

Taku Arm in clear, calm weather

Thunderheads sweeping down Taku Arm

marshy areas. One of the few places you have to watch the bottom is near the entrance of Deep Bay where islands stand in the middle of the lake. There are pinnacles sticking up that lead from the shore to the islands, and can be easily avoided by watching for them in the clear water.

The beauty along upper Taku Arm is so constant, yet changing, that it is easy to take it for granted. It is not the rugged, spectacular beauty of the lower end, nor the Switzerland-type of scenery around Atlin. Rather it is a subtle beauty with modest mountains undulating into the distance and thick forests of spruce and willow interlaced by small streams and game trails. On a calm day the mountains and trees reflect themselves perfectly in the water and the color of the water turns the reflected sky into a deeper blue-green with the clouds standing out in bold relief. It is like looking into a sky through polarized glasses.

One of the several side hikes available from the lake—perhaps the best—is up Racine River to Racine Lake. The river ends with a big noise as it tumbles down to form Racine Falls less than 200 feet from the lake. A trail leads up from an old dock to a viewpoint directly in front of the falls with spray washing over you as

Racine Falls on Taku Arm

By Lake to Tagish

you watch the different shapes the water takes in its tumble. The trail winds through beaver-thinned forests to the lake and across a flume dug there years ago for a power project that has been long abandoned.

Other side hikes can be made on old trails to Fan Tail Lake and Tutshi Lake. These are not maintained and are grown over except where animals have kept them open.

This brings up the subject of bears. There are various opinions on the wisdom of carrying a high-powered rifle while traveling in grizzly and brown bear country. Some argue it is foolish to go unarmed into the northern wilderness; others argue the opposite. Many naturalists have never carried a firearm while traveling up there; they credit noise with keeping themselves out of trouble. They carry bells on their packs or something of that nature to be sure they do not surprise a bear.

The choice is for each individual to make, but it cannot be overemphasized that those carrying a rifle should know how to use it properly. An inexperienced marksman, or careless one, can cause more trouble than an unarmed hiker who heads for a tree. A wounded bear is an incredibly mean bear, and a companion accidentally shot—or a wounded lone traveler—is a prospect too grim to contemplate. The question of firearms is a problem to be resolved by each individual.

As Taku Arm nears Tagish Lake, the mountains gradually flatten out and become gray and barren. There is virtually no vegetation growing on them, and the forest runs to their bases and suddenly stops. These low, granite mountains are characteristic of the Tagish to Lake Laberge area, and no high mountains are seen again until the section of river below Laberge.

4

Tagish to Hootalinqua

Marsh Lake begins just below the town of Tagish, and is a shallow, warm 20-mile-long and two-mile wide body of water that is the last in the chain before reaching the Yukon River.

Marsh Lake, The Yukon River to Whitehorse

Marsh Lake is sneered at by wilderness buffs because the Alaska Highway runs along its east shore and houses are frequent along that side. It is something of the ugly duckling of the headwater system and more often spoken of as an inconvenience than a place of beauty.

Of course it isn't as ugly as most chroniclers would have us

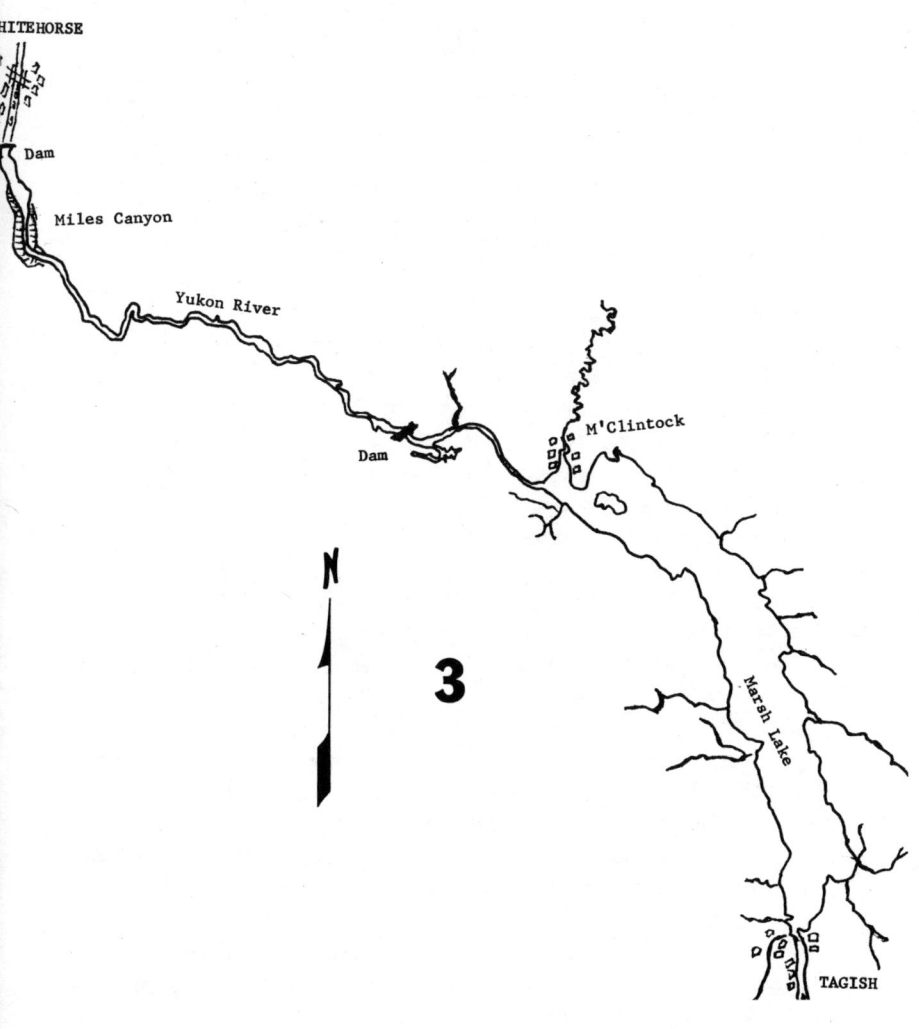

believe. It has a subdued beauty of its own, though, and by following the west shore, the noise and dust and signs of population are avoided. There are good campsites on the shore, especially at Sand Point, a peninsula of sand protruding out into the lake with a sheltered cove on the north side.

Don't be surprised if you see water skiers on the lake near the northern end where the settlement of M'Clintock has grown up. The shallow water is warmer than the other lakes, and in warm weather the hardy can be seen criss-crossing their wakes with a minimum of goosepimples.

A few miles before the Yukon River begins, the cutbanks and sweepers that so characterize the river can be seen on the west side where banks have crumbled into the water. It serves as an introduction to the river.

When the river begins, it meanders through low, marshy spots before flowing into the small lake behind the dam at the highway crossing. There are numerous sloughs and islands along this stretch of river and it is easy to wander out of the main current into the still backwaters.

The dam is known locally as the Marsh Lake Dam although it is not at the lake. It was built to help the steamboats begin running early in the summer each year by flushing the ice out of the river below the dam, and out of Lake Laberge. Now it is used as part of the flood control system and to adjust the level of Lake Schwatka behind the hydroelectric dam at Whitehorse.

A self-operating lock is at the right, or east, side of the dam, and the lock will hold four or five small boats at a time. The lock has simple instructions and requires no special education to operate. When leaving the lock, it is best to paddle directly out into the main current to avoid a back eddy directly ahead of the lock.

For the next six miles the river meanders gracefully through dense undergrowth and past cutbanks and sweepers. The river gradually narrows, then swings through a wide valley only to become enclosed again. It winds around several S-turns and power boats should follow the outer turns against the high banks to avoid hitting bottom.

About a mile above Miles Canyon is a sign identifying a flat area covered with dense vegetation as "Canyon City." Little

Miles Canyon (Wayne Towriss, Government of the Yukon Tourism & Information Branch)

of the townsite is left except some rotten logs scattered around. But during the great stampede to the Klondike and until the WP&YR line was completed to Whitehorse, this was an important town indeed.

This is the last place boats can be taken out of the river with ease before entering Miles Canyon. Even though the canyon has been partially tamed by the Whitehorse dam, the speed of the river is noticeably faster the closer you get to the canyon. Before the dam was built, the water was ferocious for a five-mile stretch. It was compressed into such a small space that it crested about three feet high in the center, created two whirlpools at the end of the canyon, then dropped down into Whitehorse Rapids, which had high stands of water that looked like galloping white horses with manes flying. It still wasn't through. Just below Whitehorse Rapids was another set called Squaw Rapids with boulders poking ominously above the surface.

Breakup time is always treacherous on the Yukon River, and travel must cease on the river during both freezeup and breakup. This photo was taken April 27, 1898, at Whitehorse Rapids.

Some of the early arrivals tried running the canyon and rapids with only limited success. Several stampeders were drowned and many others lost all their gear after hauling it over the passes the previous winter. That changed when the Mounties' honcho, the famous Sam Steele, arrived. In his direct, no-nonsense and infinitely wise fashion, he laid down the law of the canyon:

> No women or children were permitted to run the rapids; no boats would go through until the Mounties determined they were safe; no boat with people in them unless the Mounties were sure they were manned by competent men. Violators would be fined $100.

Some men hired on as guides through the canyon and rapids, under the approving eye of the Mounties (and there is nothing to the story that Jack London made a small fortune as a Miles Canyon guide. He and his partners shot the rapids and barely made it through Lake Laberge before freezeup in 1897 and wintered on the Stewart River).

Tagish to Hootalinqua

Most stampeders hauled their boats to the bank at Canyon City and began the tiresome business of portaging their gear five miles over the rugged terrain to where Whitehorse now stands, then lined their boats through the canyon and over the rapids.

However, an enterprising man named Norman Maculay had a better idea. He built a wooden-railed tramway from Canyon City over the hills to the foot of the rapids, bought some horses and made a small fortune at $25 a boatload.

The canyon and rapids also served as a definite transportation barrier between the upper lakes and the river. Steamboats built at Lake Bennett for the gold rush went down the river through the canyon and never returned; no boat was powerful enough to go back upstream.

Thus, the city of Whitehorse was born. The railroad ended and the river navigation began there.

Today, running Miles Canyon presents little difficulty. There is only a hint of the whirlpools and the crest in the center has been

After the ice cleared, the boats began running Whitehorse Rapids, a few of which made it safely after shipping several gallons of water.

flattened out by the dam backwaters. A white footbridge spans the 50-foot canyon and as you pass through it you can see hundreds of swallow nests stuck to the basalt walls.

After going through the canyon, you immediately enter Lake Schwatka, named for the American army officer who led an expedition over the passes and down the Yukon River in 1883 and presented several geographical features with names that stuck, among them Miles Canyon in honor of his commanding officer, Brig. Gen. Nelson A. Miles of Vancouver Barracks, Washington.

At the end of the lake, just above the dam, is a government dock used by both boats and seaplanes. Here you can dock and arrange for transportation around the dam. If you have rented canoes in Whitehorse, the rental agency will take care of the portage, and local taxicab companies can haul other smaller boats around, such as canoes and kayaks.

Whitehorse is the capital of the Yukon and its largest city with some 12,000 residents, or more than half the total Yukon population. It has all the conveniences of home: department stores, Colonel Sanders, Dairy Queen, a coin-operated laundromat, several hotels, restaurants—the works. You will be able to buy nearly anything you need for the rest of the trip here (with the exception of highly specialized items such as certain camera parts, etc.) and the grocery stores are accustomed to serving wilderness expeditions.

It is best to buy everything you'll need for the rest of the trip in Whitehorse, then pick up perishables and fuel at Carmacks 200 miles downstream. Freeze-dried and dehydrated food is available in Whitehorse, if you must be concerned with weight and bulk, and you can replace items that might have worn out or been demolished on the lakes.

The easiest place to reenter the river is downstream about 100 yards from the WP&YR depot.

There are two items you should be sure and add to your list at Whitehorse: A water jug and water-purification tablets. The river below Whitehorse to the end of Lake Laberge is polluted from Whitehorse sewage. It is considered potable again when the river leaves Laberge, but in the lake itself, it is a drink-at-your-own risk proposition.

Whitehorse to Hootalinqua

Many older maps show the river from Marsh Lake to Lower Laberge as the Lewes River, then from Lower Laberge to Hootalinqua as the Thirtymile River. The Yukon didn't start then until the Pelly entered. Then the Yukon was moved upstream to the Teslin where it stayed until it was established that the greatest volume of water comes from the lakes rather than from the Teslin.

The river widens after leaving Whitehorse and soon becomes more than a quarter of a mile wide. The banks are low for the first few miles, then gradually rise to nearly 200 feet high in places. It picks up both speed and width after the Takhini River enters. A short distance below the Takhini's entrance is a vast burned off area, evidence of the big forest fire of 1954 when Whitehorse was threatened. The area is covered now with the beautiful purple fireweed as the forest struggles against the harsh climate and thin topsoil to return.

There are numerous potential campsites along this section of the river, but unless one camps at the Takhini River entrance where unpolluted water is available, it is best to continue on to Lake Laberge.

The river slows noticeably as it nears Lake Laberge and mudflats become more evident. To the right of the lake entrance is a low, grassy bank called Scow Point above rows of piling stubs dating back to the steamboat era. By following the lake around to the right, you can find an adequate campsite among a group of abandoned buildings beside Laberge Creek. However, for the sake of safety from the storms that sweep the lake, it is wisest to swing back around to the left and follow the west shore all the way down the lake.

A government campground is situated opposite Richtofen Island, and you can either camp here with the motorized campers, or load up on fresh water and continue down the lake or over to the island. There are some beautiful campsites along the east shore of the high-backed island that assure privacy and interesting beachcombing. The three-mile-long island was named by Schwatka in honor of one Freiherr von Richtofen of Leipsic, a prominent figure of the day in geographical circles.

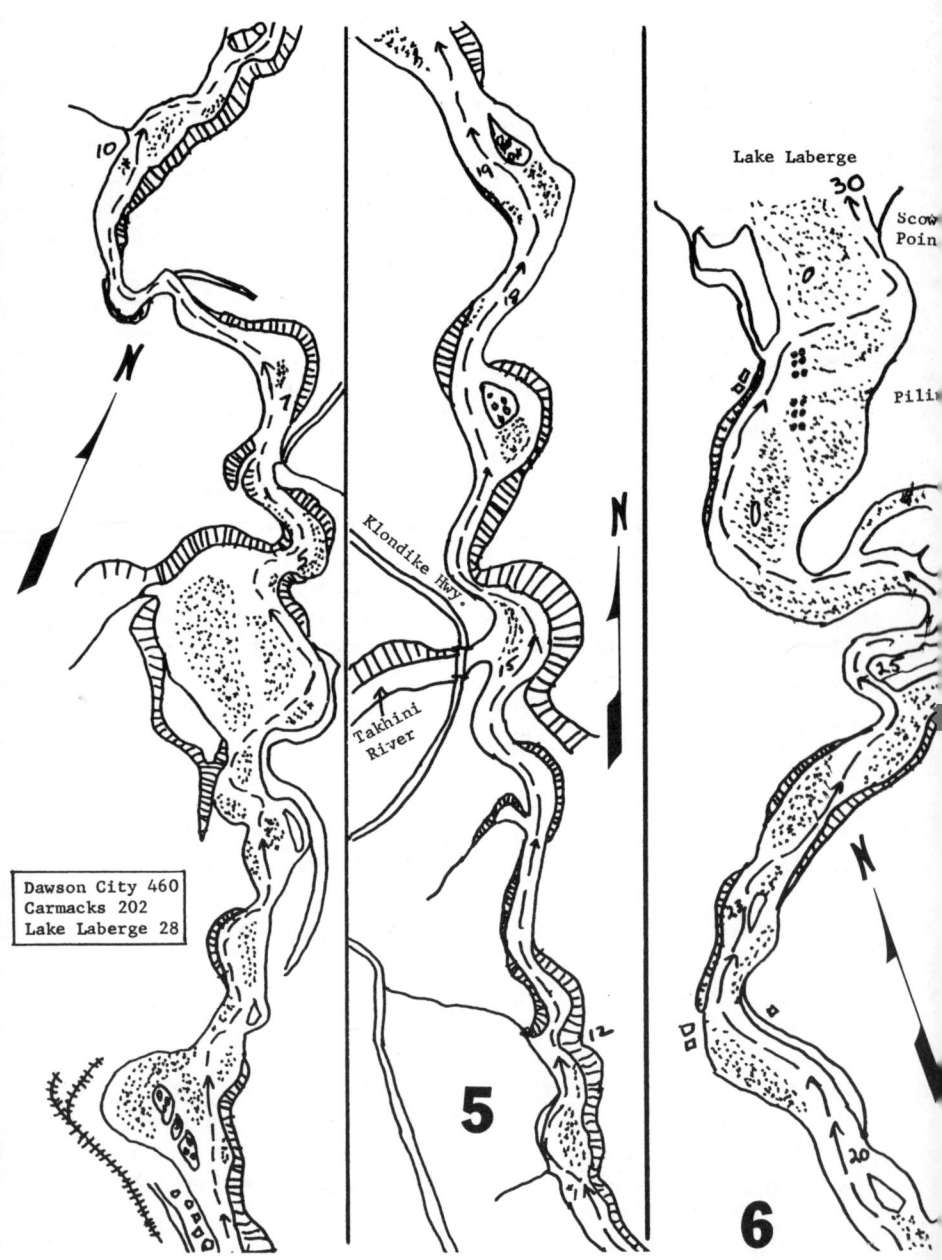

Readers of Robert Service will be more familiar with the lake than any other part of the Yukon, thanks to Service's ballad, "The Cremation of Sam McGee." The poem, like many of Service's ballads, had its conception in a very real situation. The real story (which one must assume also is subject to an embellishment here and there over the years) tells us that a rather awkward steamboat named the *Olive May* was frozen in for the winter at the head of Lake Laberge. The Mounties found that an equally frozen-in prospector who lived in a cabin near the trapped *Olive May* was dying of scurvy. A doctor was found and sent to help, but arrived too late. Since it was impossible to bury the body until the following summer, the good doctor cremated the prospector in the *Olive May's* firebox, then told an inconspicuous bank clerk named Robert Service about it. Thus is history and poetry made.

An equally touching, but infinitely less tragic story is connected with the lake's name. It was named for Mike Laberge, an explorer for the proposed Collins Telegraph line that would go across Canada and Alaska to Siberia then down to Europe; a plan that sank from history when the first trans-Atlantic cable was successfully laid.

Steamboat navigational beacon, Richtofen Island, Lake Laberge

Camping on Richtofen Island, Lake Laberge

Laberge heard of a big, beautiful lake far upstream from his camp at Selkirk and spoke of it often and wistfully, hoping he could someday see it. He never set eyes on it, but he spoke of it so often that his companions referred to it as Laberge's lake.

Traces of the Ice Ages can be seen on Richtofen Island where the glaciers left deep scars on the sloping granite boulders along the shore. During the Ice Ages the glaciers were more than a mile thick in this area, and the lake was one of those scooped out in a broad valley, again by the ice.

The surrounding countryside is similar to that around Whitehorse. The mountains are rounded, smooth and of limestone and granite. Timber and low brush grow to the lake's edge and wide expanses of sandy beaches and rocky headlands run from the water's edge to the vegetation line.

The island has numerous wild flowers during the short summer, including purple lupine, twin flower, ground cedar, northern bedstraw, fireweed, violets, creeping snowberry, Labrador-tea, mosses, lichen, memophilias, wild onion, wild rose, aspen, balsam, willow and poplar.

Children playing with old sewing machine left at Laberge Creek on Lake Laberge

From the top of Richtofen Island, looking north

At the lake's northern end, the bottom gradually rises and can be seen clearly to a depth of about 20 feet. There are numerous sand and gravel bars near the end, which must be watched for carefully in power boats, and the beginning of the river is divided into three channels. The safest route is through either the left or the center channel between the rocks, but paddled craft can go through any of the three with no danger.

Immediately after entering the swift, clear river, watch for the remains of Lower Laberge on the east side, a group of cabins back in the timber, and the hull of the steamboat *Casca*. This was one of the three boats named *Casca*, and was retired from steamer service to work as a barge before being beached to rot. This was the first *Casca* built. The second was built in Whitehorse and wrecked in 1936 in Rink Rapids. The third was built, also in Whitehorse, in 1937, then beached with the *Whitehorse* just downstream from the WP&YR depot in Whitehorse. Both burned in 1974, victims of arson.

With the burning of those two paddlewheelers, only three complete boats remain of the more than 200 that served on the river.

There is little of the lower Laberge *"Casca"* remaining today, only part of the deck and bow and some steel bolts. Back in the timber behind the sad boat are a few decaying cabins that mark the settlement of Lower Laberge. A few dog kennels, an ancient truck abandoned there and the sagging cabins remain.

The river between Lower Laberge and Hootalinqua, still locally known as the Old Thirtymile River because it is 30 miles to Hootalinqua, is swift and clear as it winds through the canyons beneath wind-carved hoodoos in the cliffs above. It is a stretch of river to be savored, and one that should be drifted as silently as possible because it is so narrow that wildlife frequently is seen along the banks less than 100 feet from the boat.

This stretch of river also is the closest to a wilderness river you will find on the Yukon; the section least touched by man during the steamboat era. Old maps show only one woodcamp along this stretch, and since it is so rugged along the banks, most of the timber is still virgin. Along the remainder of the river the timber for the most part is second-growth. In many stretches, the spruce did not regenerate itself and willows and aspen have taken over.

The steamboats had insatiable appetites for fuel and burned an

Remains of steamboat *Casca* at Lower Laberge

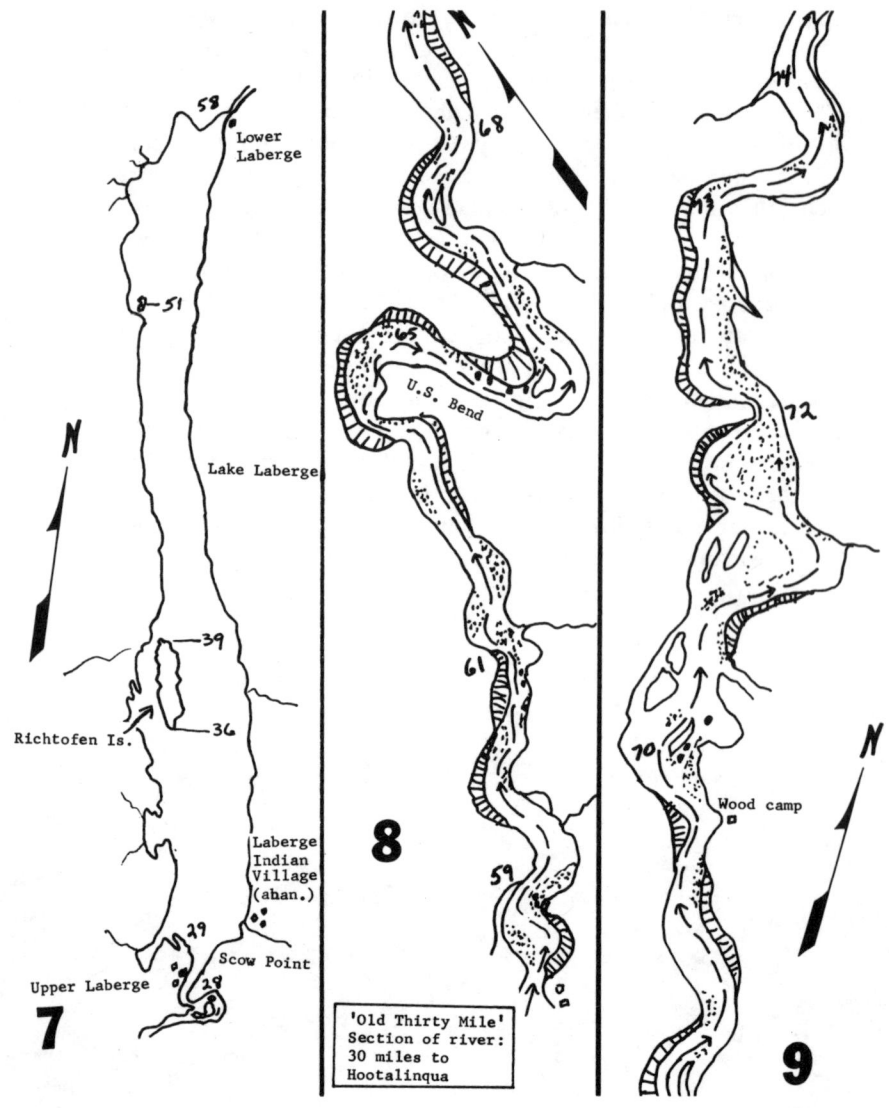

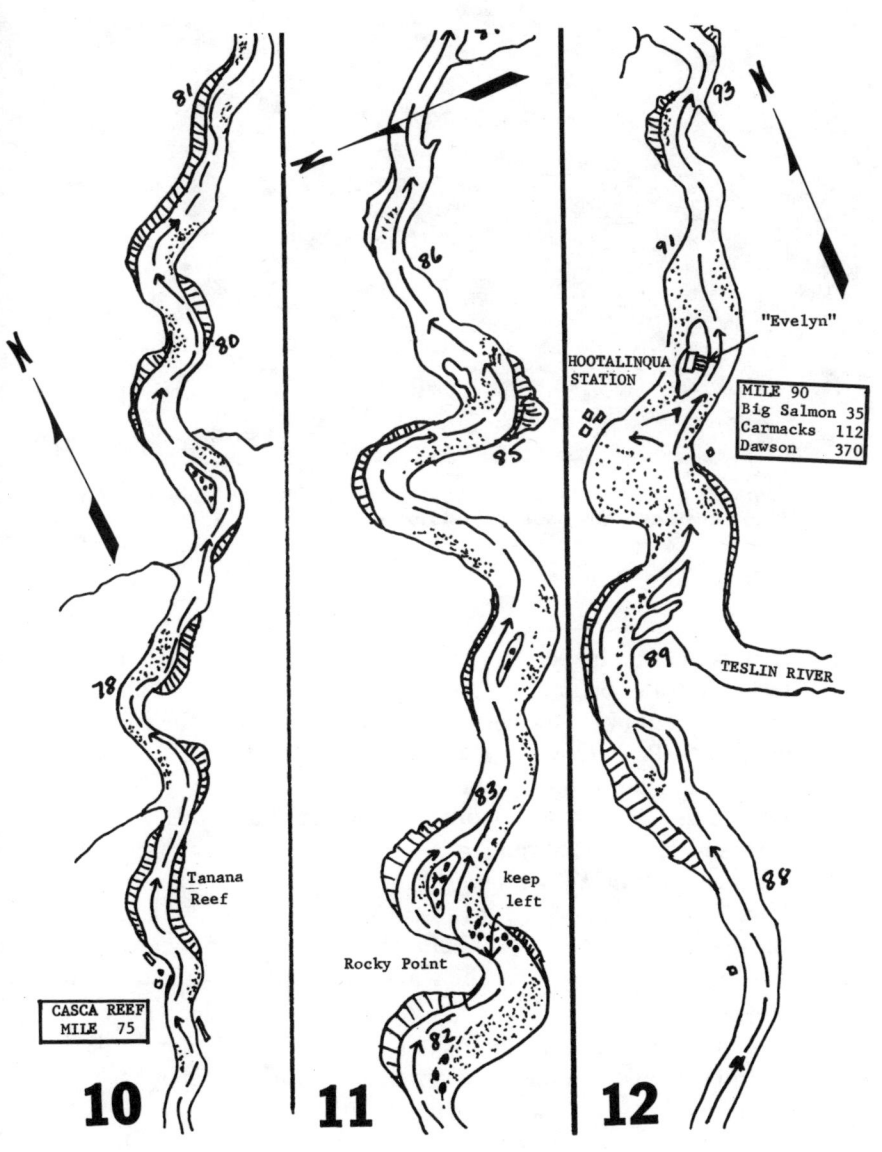

Cutbanks and erosion-carved hoo-doos along Old Thirtymile section of Yukon River between Laberge and Hootalinqua

estimated 300,000 cords of wood during the era. One could burn two cords of wood an hour, each stick four feet long, and it is little wonder that toward the end of the steamboat era on the river, the owners (WP&YR owned nearly every form of public transportation on the river, including a plane that flew between Whitehorse, Skagway and Juneau) converted to oil. Woodcutter camps were stationed roughly every 30 miles along the river and contractors with WP&YR were paid $8 to $10 a cord; some contractors paid men $5 a cord to cut it for them. The green wood was stacked to dry for a year before being used. Some woodcutters ran small traplines during the winter, but the sawing and cutting was a full-time if lonely occupation.

While this section of the river is called the Old Thirtymile, it should be noted that the usual system of naming rivers by the mile ordinarily took another form. When the trio of traders—Jack McQuesten, Arthur Harper and Al Mayo—joined forces to support the prospectors until the big strike, they established a trading post called Fort Reliance in 1874 six miles downstream from

Tagish to Hootalinqua

where Dawson City stands today, heartbreakingly close to the big strike that wasn't to be until 22 years later.

Since Fort Reliance was the first post that far upriver into what is now Canada, streams often were named for their distance from the fort, hence the Forty Mile, the Sixty Mile, etc. In most cases, those original names remain on all maps, sometimes as one word (Fortymile) or two (Forty Mile).

An outstanding feature of the Thirtymile is US Bend, about seven miles from Lower Laberge. The clear, clean water bores rapidly through a channel carved in a sharp S-curve with high bluffs on either side.

A few streams enter the river along this portion, all potable as is the river itself. The pollution from Whitehorse dissipates in Lake Laberge and the river emerges clean again.

Campsites are easily found along this portion of the river and wildlife—moose, bears, eagles, ravens and swallows by the thousand—are frequently seen. The area lends itself to short side hikes to the top of bluffs for views up and down the river.

During the gold rush this trio was swamped between the outlet of Lake Laberge and Hootalinqua on the old Thirtymile River.

Hootalinqua, at the junction of Yukon River and Teslin River

The Thirtymile ends at Hootalinqua, where the broad Teslin enters. A wide clearing and excellent campsite are on the left (west) bank overlooking the rivers and a slough where arctic grayling and pike can be easily caught for dinner. Hootalinqua was a RCMP post with two of the buildings still standing that offer some protection from the weather.

5

Hootalinqua to Fort Selkirk

The river gains both momentum and silt with the Teslin's entrance, and it becomes progressively browner as it progresses to the north. However, it is still potable. For the start from Hootalinqua see map strip 12.

Immediately downstream from Hootalinqua is an island you should visit, called Shipyard Island on some maps but named Hootalinqua Island by a sign on the island. In the middle of the island is an old, decaying steamboat named the *Evelyn* which was pulled up on the ways for repair and left there forever after WP&YR bought it from its bankrupt owners but never used it. Originally the vessel was named the *Evelyn* and was built in Seattle for the Upper Tanana Trading Co. in 1908. It was wrecked in the Tanana and taken down to St. Michael's boatyard and a new hull built. Then it was sold to the North Ameri-

Abandoned steamboat *Evelyn* on Hootalinqua Island

can Transportation & Trading Co. and renamed the *Norcom*. But somewhere along the line its original name was used again, and it is so-named by a sign on its hull today.

A few miles further downstream is the wreck of the steamer, *Klondike*, the first one under that name, which was wrecked in the Thirtymile River in 1936 and drifted to her present location. Its skeleton sticks up above the water during late summer but often is covered during high-water periods.

Hootalinqua to Little Salmon

After leaving Hootalinqua, the river valley opens up considerably and the cutbanks on one side, willow-covered lowlands on the other, become common. An occasional whirlpool occurs but presents no danger; just a brisk diversion from the normal, swift river with occasional upwells from the rocks on the bottom.

The village of Big Salmon is on the east side of the river 35 miles downstream from Hootalinqua where a river of the same name enters. It was a trading post and Indian village when traffic was on the river, and buildings are still standing on both sides of the river. The abandoned buildings are adequate for some protection, and often boaters pitch their tents outside for sleeping and use one of the buildings of this and other villages for cooking. By setting fire to a mosquito coil (and being absolutely certain it is placed on a piece of metal so it won't set fire to the building itself), you can clear mosquitos quite rapidly from a room.

All villages along the river are protected by the territorial government and nobody should have to be discouraged from defacing or destroying any of the structures. Extreme care should always be taken to avoid fires. Furniture and planks should not be ripped off anywhere and used for firewood. There always are adequate supplies of downed timber and branches for open campfires, but sometimes you will have to walk a few feet to get them.

When approaching these villages that almost always are at the mouth of a stream, whether in a power or paddle situation, it is best to head for the slack or backwater that usually results when the entering river sweeps out into the main channel. It can be

Shower at Big Salmon, ghost town

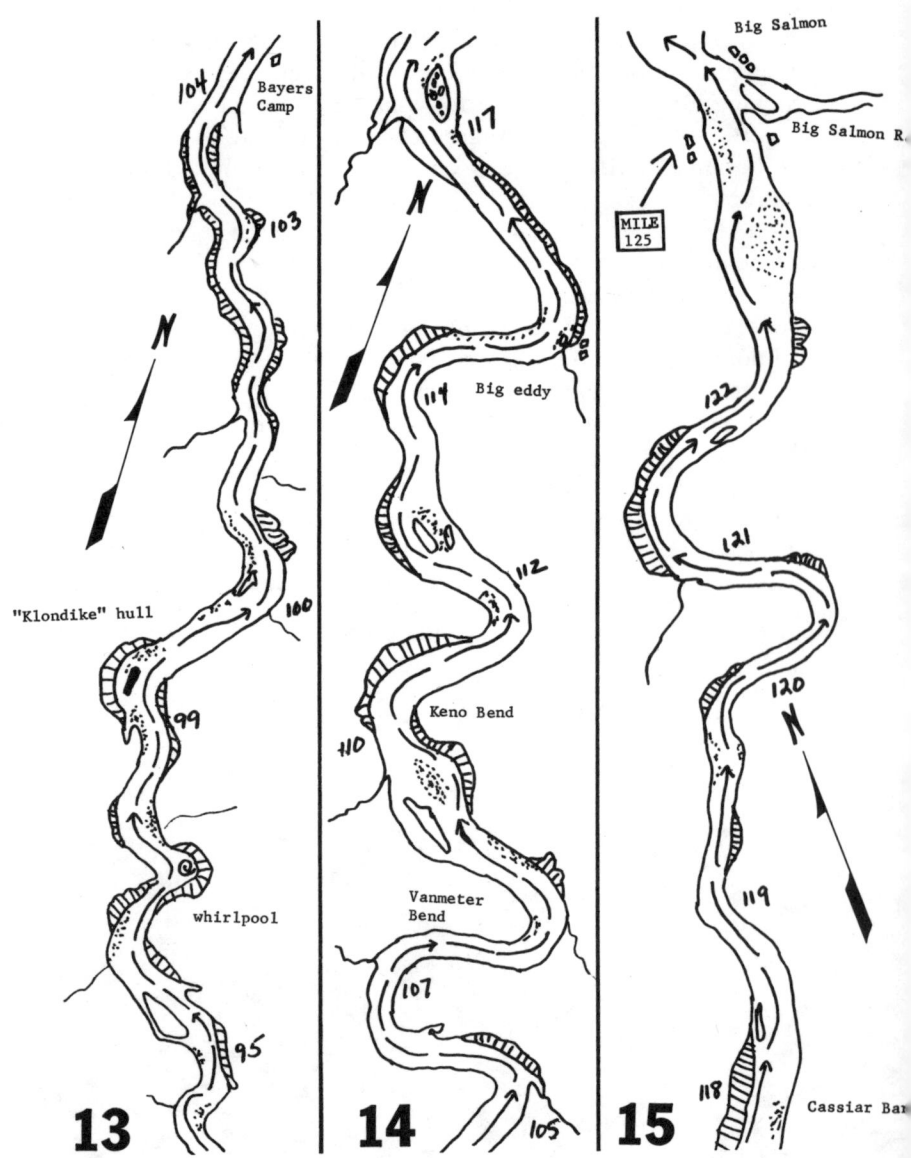

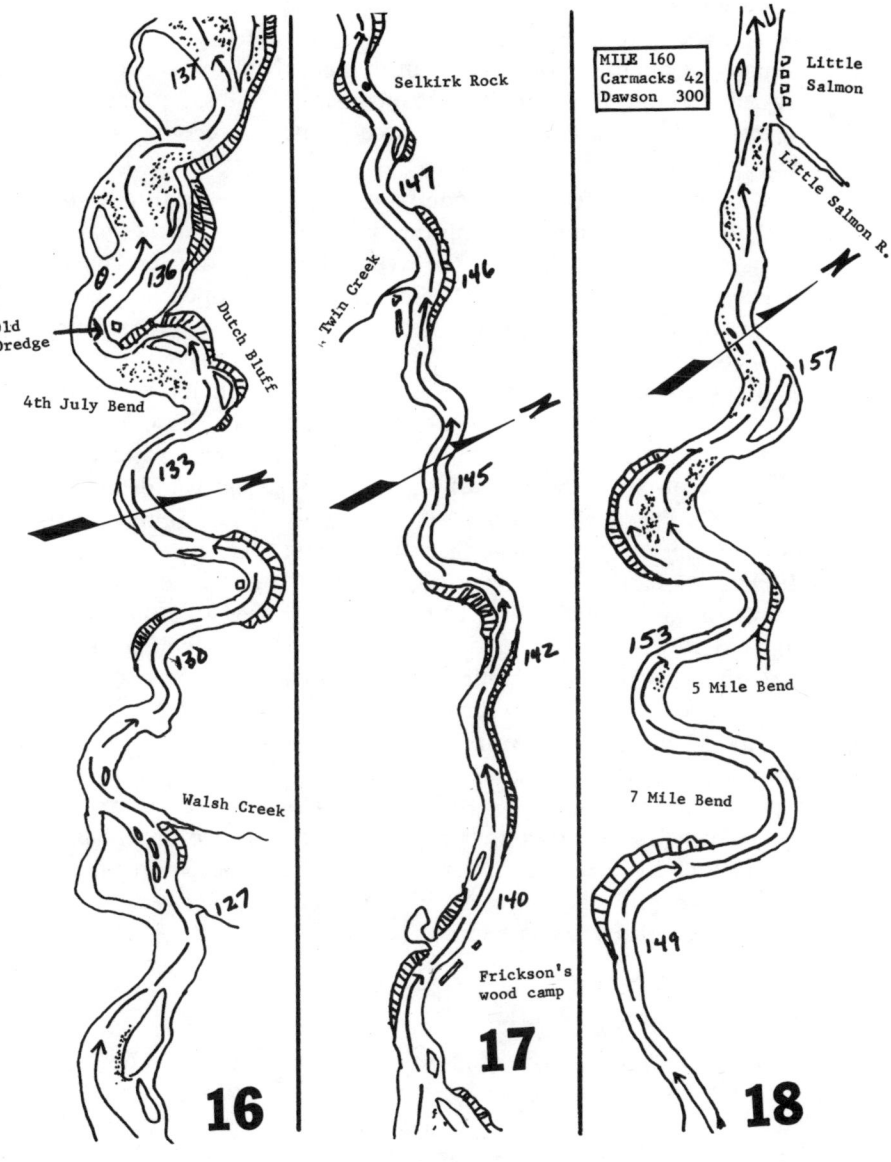

tricky and hard work for a paddler but should present no problem for a power boat so long as you don't ding a propeller on a rock near the shore. With a power boat it is best to go slightly beyond the point you plan to land, then ease slowly upstream and into the bank. This is much easier and safer than the intentional collisions you often see boaters executing when heading for shore in swift water.

Unless you prefer lots of company on the river, it usually is best to plan on camping along the bank or on one of the many islands that appear all along the river. There is always an abundance of driftwood on the islands for fires and open, exposed sandbars where the wind will keep mosquitos away from your stew. Some residents say mosquitos in your stew or your coffee add protein to your diet. Perhaps so, but they don't say anything about them having a jolly effect on your disposition.

It is 35 miles from Big Salmon to Little Salmon, and you should plan stops at each of the old towns and woodcutter's camps for the sake of curiosity if nothing else. Little Salmon is a smaller cluster of buildings than Big Salmon, but it has a small Indian cemetery of special interest. Here are a group of the small wooden "spirit houses" built over graves with windows and articles of clothing and household goods that belonged to the person buried there. One cabin, or spirit house, has several toys inside which would indicate a child was buried there.

About 10 miles downstream from Big Salmon is an old dredge on the right, or east bank, that was abandoned years ago. It was hauled up and down the river by its owners to dredge for gold on the feeder streams. Not, as some assume, to dredge the river itself to keep the channels open. That type of dredging, along with pile dikes and other Corps of Engineer trappings, was never introduced on the river.

Little Salmon to Carmacks

This stretch of the river (map strip 19 continues on from strip 18) has lost something of its feeling of isolation because the Whitehorse-to-Dawson City highway can be seen on the eastern slopes of the hills from many stretches of the river.

The presence of the highway and power lines immediately

Spirit houses at Indian cemetery, Little Salmon

puts you back into the feeling that civilization is nearby. Too nearby, perhaps? Whatever effect it has on you, there are interesting stretches of river on the way to Carmacks.

The number of islands increases considerably and during the high-water periods they will remind you of steamboats because they have what amounts to bow waves as the rushing river hits their prow and splashes upward on the rocks and driftwood that inevitably gather there.

A nice side hike can be taken from the site of Lakeview up the small stream on an old trail. The stream has an abundance of grayling and pike which can be caught in the stream or where it enters the river. From Teslin down, the only places where fishing can be worth the effort is where the streams enter the silt-laden river, or up the larger streams.

Other side hikes can be taken up to the top of the bald knobs on either side of the river, some of which are up to 2,000 feet high.

As you approach Carmacks, the highway remains in sight most of the time, and the Tantalus Butte coal mine comes into view on the east side. The butte was named by Schwatka during his journey downstream. He wrote that "a conspicuous bald butte

Abandoned gold dredge on Yukon River

could be seen directly in front of our raft no less than seven times, on as many different stretches of the river. I called it Tantalus Butte and was glad to see it disappear from sight."

In Greek mythology Tantalus was king of Phrygia, son of Zeus and the nymph Pluto. He served the flesh of his son, Pelops, to the gods and was condemned to stand in water that receded when he tried to drink and beneath branches of fruit that always eluded his grasp.

The mine in the butte produces about 80 tons of coal daily for the dryer plant at the Anvil Mine near Faro, the largest mine in the Yukon which produces silver, lead and zinc.

It has been in operation off and on since about 1900, and the coal originally was used for heating in Dawson City and Whitehorse before the Anvil Mine Corporation bought it in the mid-1960s. Today, about a dozen miners work there, mostly Indians living in the Carmacks area.

The highway bridge at Carmacks crossed the T's and dotted the I's for the steamboat era. When it was built, there were no allowances made for the high-hatted steamboats, and when the *Keno* went on its final journey downstream to Dawson City to

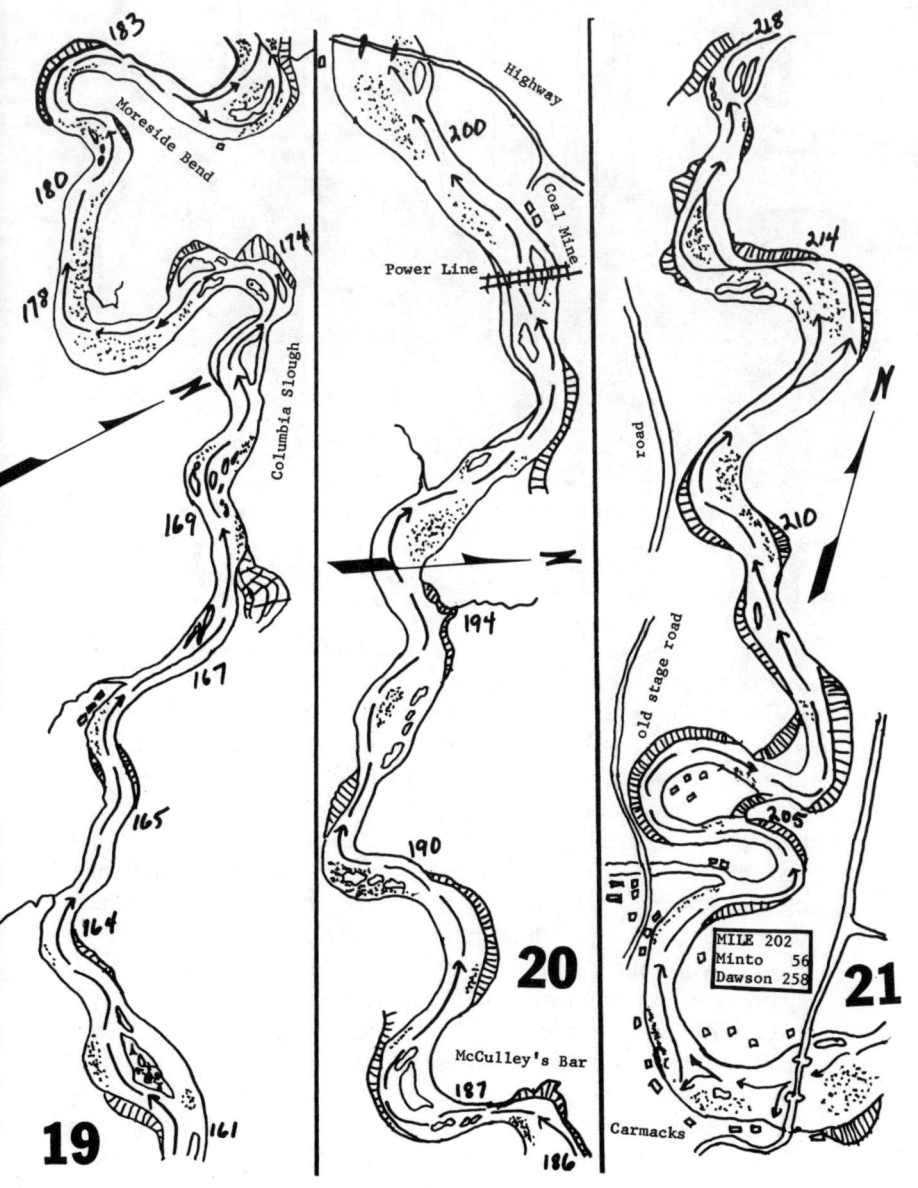

Tantalaus Butte just above Carmacks, with coal mine showing

become a museum, part of its top deck had to be removed and the stacks hinged to clear the bridge.

Carmacks has about 200 residents and is the last town you will see until Dawson City about 260 miles away. Here you will have to reprovision and top off the fuel tanks again and buy any items you might have dropped in the drink (everybody on the river loses something, it seems: gloves, sunglasses, knife, etc.). It also is your last chance for a restaurant meal and a shower. A roadhouse offers showers at $1 per person, but you should be forewarned; the mosquitos love nothing better than fresh, clean meat. So as soon as you take the shower, you'll have to make yourself rank again with repellent or live with the itchy bumps.

Unfortunately, there is no convenient place to land at Carmacks at this writing. The Forest Service has a dock on the river but using it is generally frowned upon. There also is a dock beneath the bridge but it is a far walk to town for supplies (about a half mile), so your only other alternative is to tie up to the bank as close to the town as possible, then form a fire brigade and pass the groceries and fuel down to the boats.

Hootalinqua to Fort Selkirk

If you have a large load of purchases to make, and especially if you have to refill a drum of fuel, it is best to find someone to hire transportation to the river. All stores and service stations naturally are on the highway and it is quite a walk with arms laden with goods. If you carry a backpack, it would be wise to unload it and haul your material in it.

Carmacks to Fort Selkirk

Just after leaving Carmacks (map strip 21) you will think you're suffering from some rare eye disease or that you're watching a movie and someone suddenly reversed the film. On the way into Carmacks you will see a church on the shore back in a grove of trees with a prominent cross. Then, after you leave town, you'll see the same church in the same grove of trees again.

Be not dismayed. You're going around Shirtwaste Bend, one of the sharpest bends in the river and one in which the river very nearly doubles back on itself. It also is a nifty place to

Boating downstream was a cinch, but going upstream was nothing but hard work. The river is too swift to paddle or pole against, and the boats must be tracked, one man pulling and the other pushing with a pole to keep it away from the bank.

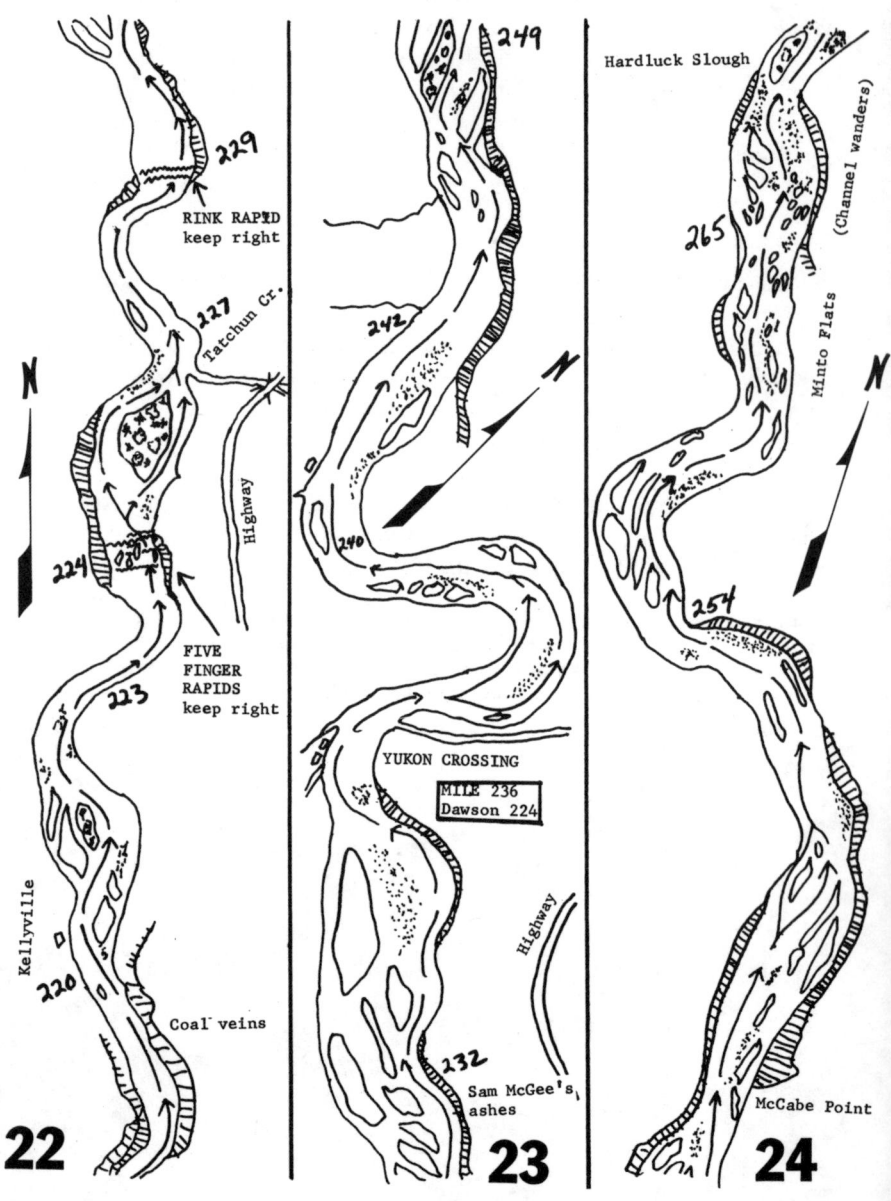

Hootalinqua to Fort Selkirk

completely lose your sense of direction. However, the river soon straightens out again and heads north as it is supposed to.

The water flows rapidly along the stretch below Carmacks and down to the rapids, and is characterized by boils, surges, an occasional flat pool and riffle. It is a beautiful stretch of river with high canyon walls on either side that occasionally give way to sand and gravel bluffs directly above the river with a second and higher set of bluffs behind those.

Five Finger Rapids are about 20 miles downstream from Carmacks, and just before you reach them, you will begin seeing wind-carved hoodoos in the hillside directly above the river with swallow nesting in them.

Campsites above the rapids are a little more difficult to find than in other stretches of the river because of the high bluffs. There is an old settlement called Kellyville on the west side of the river about four miles above the rapids, but it frequently is used by Indians as a summer fish camp and should not be counted on for a campsite. It is best to watch for an exposed gravel bar or a likely knoll back in the timber if you prefer camping above the rapids and saving them for another day.

The rapids are not much by Colorado River standards. In ac-

View of Five Finger Rapids from Highway (Wayne Towriss, Government of the Yukon Tourism & Information Branch)

Flat-bottomed river boat going through Five Finger Rapids

tuality, they consist of a few bumps, some whitewater and you're out. But they should not become a toy, either, because they can tip a canoe or kayak easily and the combination of cold water and the prospect of losing one's provisions should not be overlooked.

Five Finger Rapids get their name from the four "flower pot" islands in the river and the five channels of water that go around them. The islands are unique on the river; that type does not appear elsewhere. The proper approach is to the extreme right, or east channel, since it is the safest and widest. Steamboats always used this channel and the transportation companies anchored a heavy cable in a shack just above the rapids (which is still there but few see it because they're watching the water, not the bank), and the steamboat crewmen would hook the cable to a winch on the bow, then winch themselves up through the swift water.

Hootalinqua to Fort Selkirk

There is a good chance you will have an audience as you navigate Five Fingers because the highway runs high up on the cliff above them and a turnout has been built there for a panoramic view of the rapids and river.

The rapids consist of two-foot waves with strong back eddies on either side caused by the water rushing around the islands. There is also a slight crosscurrent caused by the water dashing against the right-hand cliff, then being forced out across the main channel. You should enter the rapids in the center to avoid both the crosscurrent and the back eddies below the rapids.

A short distance below the rapids is a government campground on the short Tatchun Creek. A road leads from the creek mouth back to the campground and across the highway to Tachun Lake. During July and August many salmon are caught in the river at the creek mouth.

Rink Rapids is six miles downstream and here again the right side should be taken. By bearing right, the rapids themselves can be missed entirely and only choppy water will be encountered. During the steamboat era, Rink Rapids were much rougher than they are now, a situation that was altered by putting some dynamite in the rapids and blasting away. The rapids themselves are not especially dangerous and many boaters, seeking one last thrill before the flat water below, run through

Boat entering Five Finger Rapids

Fisherman hauling in salmon at Tatchun Creek just below Five Finger.

the middle. However, as with any set of rapids, you should pull over to shore above and scout them before committing yourself to a course without knowing what lies ahead.

After Rink Rapids, the river flattens out considerably and the current slows to about half speed, or around three miles an hour. The valley floor becomes wider and the banks lower. More

Volcanic ash deposit below Rink Rapids called Sam McGee's Ashes

islands appear and you have only shallow water or dead-end sloughs to watch for while navigating this portion.

Just below Rink Rapids is a deep deposit of volcanic ash in the bank that has been named "Sam McGee's Ashes," although old Sam, as noted earlier, was cremated far upstream at Lake Laberge.

Such ash deposits are seen elsewhere along the bank, usually in the form of a layer up to a foot deep. The deposit came from eruptions far to the west in the St. Elias Range, one of which covered all the area now occupied by Whitehorse. So poor is the soil in Whitehorse, and a few other places in the Yukon, that topsoil is often imported for lawns and gardens.

By watching the river bank, you will see how shallow the topsoil is all along the river, which in part explains why the timber does not reach marketable size in the Yukon's interior. Other factors, of course, include the extremely cold winters and the semiarid climate that retards decomposition. But the Yukon has not had sufficient time from the last Ice Age to build up a deep topsoil above the permafrost which is evident in varying depths throughout most of the Yukon.

Four miles below "Sam McGee's Ashes" is the ghost town of Yukon Crossing, which gives an excellent example of pioneer architecture in the two-story log cabin roadhouse. The roadhouse served both the river traffic in the summer and the winter-road traffic during the other 9 months of the year.

The government cleared and maintained a road of sorts that ran from Whitehorse to Dawson City along a route similar to the highway right-of-way today. It crossed the river at Yukon Crossing, followed it down to the Pelly River, then swung inland in a more or less straight line to Dawson City.

Dogs, then horses and finally small Caterpillars were used to pull sleds and wagons during the winter. Passengers were expected to be warmly dressed, hardy and uncomplaining.

Below Yukon Crossing the river widens and flattens even more as it enters Minto Flats. Islands become more frequent and it is often difficult to tell which is an island and which is the mainland. These characteristics continue well below the town of Minto, then the river narrows again and picks up speed when the Pelly joins it.

There isn't much at Minto of interest to the wilderness buff. There are some pit toilets near the river bank for those who consider that sort of thing a rare luxury, and there are a few picnic

Undercut bank sloughing off into the river

Yukon Crossing. Two-story roadhouse in background.

tables and fire pits scattered around the open field that leads back to the abandoned buildings of Minto.

Minto originally was an Indian village, and the houses and caches are still used by descendants during the salmon runs. The town has the distinction of having a series of unsolved murders in the early 1950s.

Minto has an emergency airstrip and helicopters as well as fixed-wing planes frequently use it as a refueling station, as evidenced by stacks of orange barrels around the river bank. The highway is a short distance up a dirt road.

The remaining 24 miles to Fort Selkirk are more of the same—a wide river with many islands and an occasional glimpse of the old winter road going across a hillside on the east bank of the river. After leaving Minto, all traces of the highway disappear and that evidence of civilization will not be seen again until Dawson City.

The landscape beside the river slowly rises from Minto to the confluence of the Pelly at Fort Selkirk and high banks gradually grow higher while the river is broad and island-dotted.

One of the visual treats of the river trip is to approach Fort Selkirk late at night when the sun lies low over the river and its slanting light hits the windows of the town like lamps burning in the windows of a small coastal town. No matter the time of day one arrives, there is something welcoming about the town and many boaters spend an extra day there, getting their land legs back again, catching up on laundry and strolling around the clearing on the high bank above the river with a view back up the Yukon and across to the Pelly and the high, basalt cliff that defines the river on the other side.

The best landing site is toward the north end of the town at a ramp carved into the high bank during the steamboat era. Watch for the schoolhouse, the closest building to the bank, and you will see the ramp directly below it. The river is swift along the bank and requires some exertion for canoeists or kayakers to stop or slow enough to leap out and haul the craft in.

Selkirk (many drop the Fort from its title) is the best preserved town along the river and the largest. It is in good shape because Danny Roberts, his wife and daughter live there and he serves as

Minto. Large cache in background.

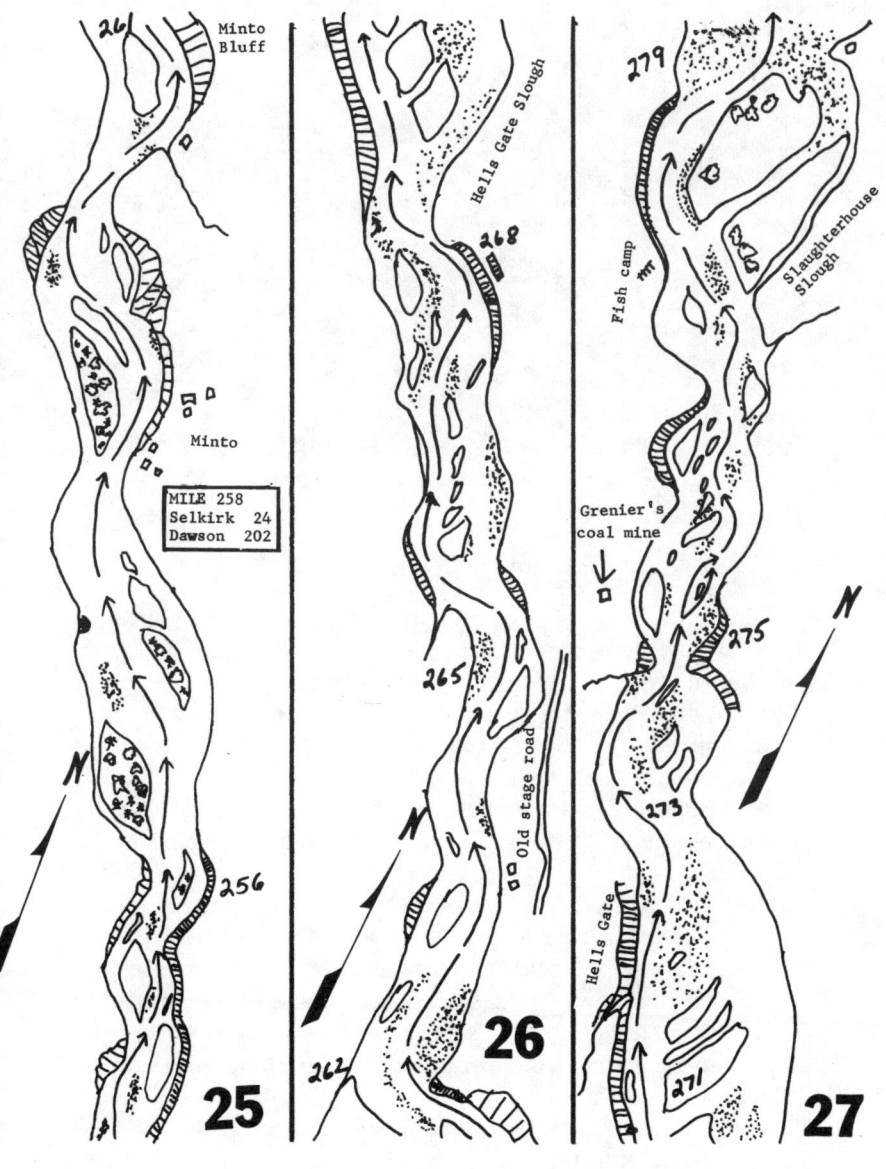

Fort Selkirk at nearly midnight in June

watchman and caretaker. You will meet Danny shortly after arrival because he is required to have every visitor sign a register, and he will point out the best sources of firewood and the buildings that offer the most protection from weather.

Just outside the schoolhouse is a big firepit for your convenience. Visitors are welcome to use any of the buildings as sleeping quarters, with the obvious understanding that the buildings are not to be littered and anything found inside them stays inside them.

One of the more interesting aspects of the Yukon River's evacuation during the 1950s is shown at Selkirk. When the people left the river and moved to the towns along the highway, most of them left behind their china, stoves, furniture, curtains and drapes and bedding. The freight rates on the steamboats were so high that it was cheaper to leave them and replace everything from stores in Whitehorse and Dawson City.

Until the past few years after boaters started using the river again, and helping themselves to what was not theirs, it wasn't unusual to walk into one of the unlocked houses and find tables

Fort Selkirk mission church in background

set as if for company, pots and pans gleaming from their pegs in the kitchen and stoves banked for fire with more firewood in containers behind the stoves.

Before the advent of recreational boaters from outside the Yukon drainage system, these houses were used by people on the river as way stations, and the dictates of the North—that you leave the place clean, replace any food you may have eaten and leave a fire ready to light—remained much in effect. Some removed items from the houses and buildings as they were needed, but the unspoken, strong law was very much in effect.

Fort Selkirk was founded by Robert Campbell of the Hudson's Bay Co. in 1848. After Campbell and his companions built Fort Selkirk and set up a trading post with the local Indians, life fell into a relatively normal pattern and they seemed content. They had no difficulty in obtaining ample food for the winters with fish easily netted in the backwaters of a slough near the post, and moose and caribou in abundant supply back in the forest.

But they had made an enemy in the case of the Chilkat Indians, far to the south on Lynn Canal in what is now Alaska. The Chilkats had exercised a monopoly on the Interior Indians. Some had visited the post during the four years it had existed and had

Danny Roberts, caretaker at Fort Selkirk

Fort Selkirk

never shown particularly good manners while there. Their resentment was a matter of record and it made not only Campbell and his men nervous, it frightened the local Indians.

On the morning of August 20, 1852, Campbell and three men were cutting the tall native grass that grows abundantly there for the post's milk cow. They saw five rafts bearing down on the post with 27 Chilkats aboard.

They came ashore armed with guns and three of Campbell's employees headed for the timber behind the post, leaving Campbell and two others to face the Chilkats. He tried diplomacy, which was ineffective, but the Chilkats did not attack that day. Instead, they permitted Campbell and his crew to go to bed that night while "the infernal devils" prowled the post all night

Interior of house with water pump at Fort Selkirk

Indian cemetery at Fort Selkirk

trying to break into the buildings through locked doors and barred windows.

The next afternoon two hunters and their families returned to the post from a hunting trip up the Pelly, and before they could escape, the Chilkats had waded out into the swift water to grab the boat and pull it ashore.

This action seemed to set them off, especially after two Indians working for Campbell disarmed two Chilkats. The battle was on. Several of them rushed Campbell, whose life was saved at the first by two rifles that misfired. There were so many on him that the Indians got in each other's way and could neither shoot nor stab him with their knives.

Inexplicably, when they had wrestled him to the river bank, he was released. He and a few others managed to get into their boats and head downstream to the HBC's next post at Fort Yukon. After Campbell's undignified departure the Chilkats burned the post. Then began the most remarkable hike on record. Campbell walked back to Fort Simpson, where the Liard River meets the Mackenzie. He hoped to get permission to reestablish Fort Selkirk, but nobody could give him that power. So, in the middle of the winter, he struck out over the mountains on snowshoes to Fort Garry (now Winnipeg, Manitoba) and again was rebuffed. Still determined, he snowshoed on down to Minnesota to board a train to headquarters in Montreal.

By the time he reached Fort Garry, he had hiked more than 2000 miles across several mountain ranges, including the awesome Rockies. And all for naught; the company would not honor his request to rebuild Selkirk.

The post lay silent until the Klondike gold rush, when the Canadian government sent a company from the Yukon Field Force, a special unit, there with the RCMP. A town grew there, and before it was abandoned for the highway in the early 1950s, some 200 people resided there.

Now the town consists of the schoolhouse, an Anglican church and minister's home, a Taylor & Drury store, a few sturdy houses and remains of the Yukon Field Force headquarters.

Back in the timber is a Catholic church (which tells you the Anglicans were more powerful there than the Catholics) and the altar appears ready for mass to be conducted.

One of the most interesting sites around Selkirk is the large Indian cemetery near the Catholic church. One of the largest on the river, it has many graves with fences and headstones made of wood carved into unsophisticated but artistic designs.

Selkirk also was an important station in the telegraph line that ran between Whitehorse and Dawson City. Some of the poles and

River scene at night below Selkirk

General river scene showing sweepers at left, cut bank at right

insulators stuck into trees can be seen all along the route. At Selkirk, you can see boxes of the old insulators and pieces of telephones hanging on walls. When the line was in operation, men were stationed along the route and were responsible for its care. Each summer the men would walk along their lines to repair them or clear brush away from them, then catch a steamboat back home.

Directly across the river from Selkirk is the high, black basalt wall that runs downriver 12 miles and up the Pelly two or three miles, an old lava flow from a long extinct volcano. The top of the wall is decorated with aspen and birch trees, and only an occasional patch of lichen can be seen clinging to the wall itself.

It is said that several old cannonballs are scattered along its base and the wall itself is pocked from cannons that were fired from Selkirk during special ceremonies.

One further note: The Roberts family moved back to Selkirk, where both Danny and his wife were born and schooled, and they moved there for the privacy it offered. They are friendly people but, like the rest of us, don't appreciate strangers walking around their house and peering in at them. There is something

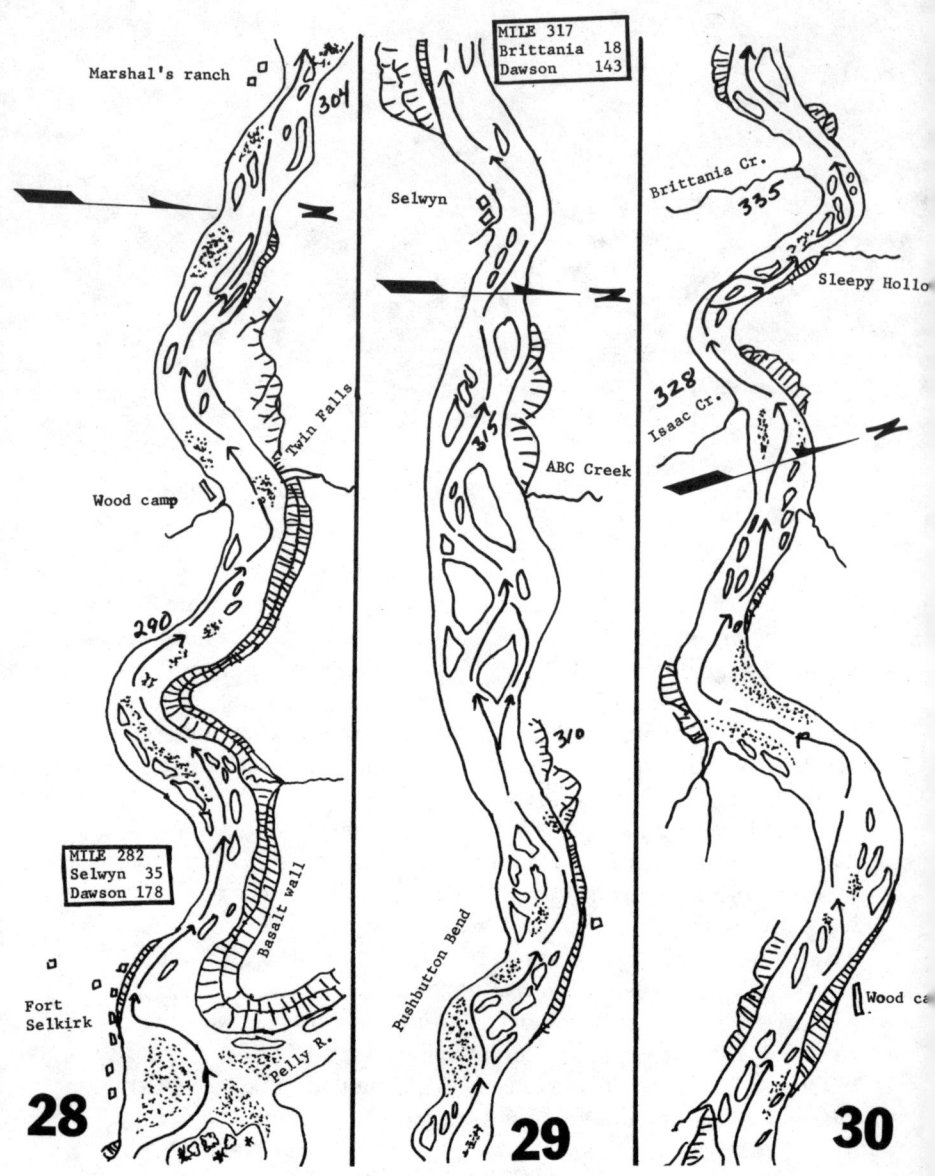

Cabin beginning to fall into river as course changed to undercut it

that gives visitors to the North the idea the local residents, espcially if they are Indian (as the Roberts are) or Eskimo, that they won't mind tourists invading their privacy and taking pictures of them without permission. It is a common ailment, but one which can be healed by asking yourself: Would I mind if someone walked into my yard, peered into my window and took pictures of my family? You might also ask yourself if you would feel any differently about it if the peerers and clickers were of a different race. say Indian or Eskimo . . .

6

Fort Selkirk to Dawson City and Journey's End

The character of the river changes considerably at Selkirk as the low, swampy banks are replaced by cliffs and mountains in the background. Geologically, this is an older section of river and has cut canyons for itself, while upstream the river apparently is younger. Some geologists believe the original river followed the Pelly down to Selkirk and that the Yukon from the lakes to Selkirk was carved out after the last Ice Age.

As you leave Selkirk (see map strip 28), you will immediately notice the canyon characteristics and a good deal of your time will be spent looking almost straight up to see over the top of the 12-mile-long basalt wall on the right (north) shore. The river cuts directly into the base of the cliffs, which sometimes rise 450 feet or more, and landing sites on that side are sparse, indeed. The main channel hugs the cliffs for the most part, and the cliffs

Cliff on lower river (below Fort Selkirk)

end 12 miles downstream at a place called Twin Falls. Apparently two waterfalls are formed there during spring melt, but they don't function during the summer months. All you can hope to see are twin stains on the cliff.

Camps, Way Stations and Creeks Below Selkirk

There are a number of old woodcutters' camps and way stations along this stretch of river. Isaac Creek was both the site of a placer mine and woodcutter camp, although the buildings have been demolished. Britannia Creek has an old road that ran up into the mountains nearly 25 miles to another placer mine. Ballarat Creek has cabins in good repair that are privately-owned and Coffee Creek was an old trading post that also has buildings, usually occupied now. A trail leads up from Coffee Creek into the mountains that was used as a route to the Chisana Gold Rush in Alaska in 1913. Since the trail hasn't been used in decades, it is mostly grown over now. A few of the cabins are used during winters by trappers.

Kirkman Creek, a former post office and small farm, is privately-owned and maintained. Obviously, one should avoid

Kirkman Creek, privately-owned and protected by government

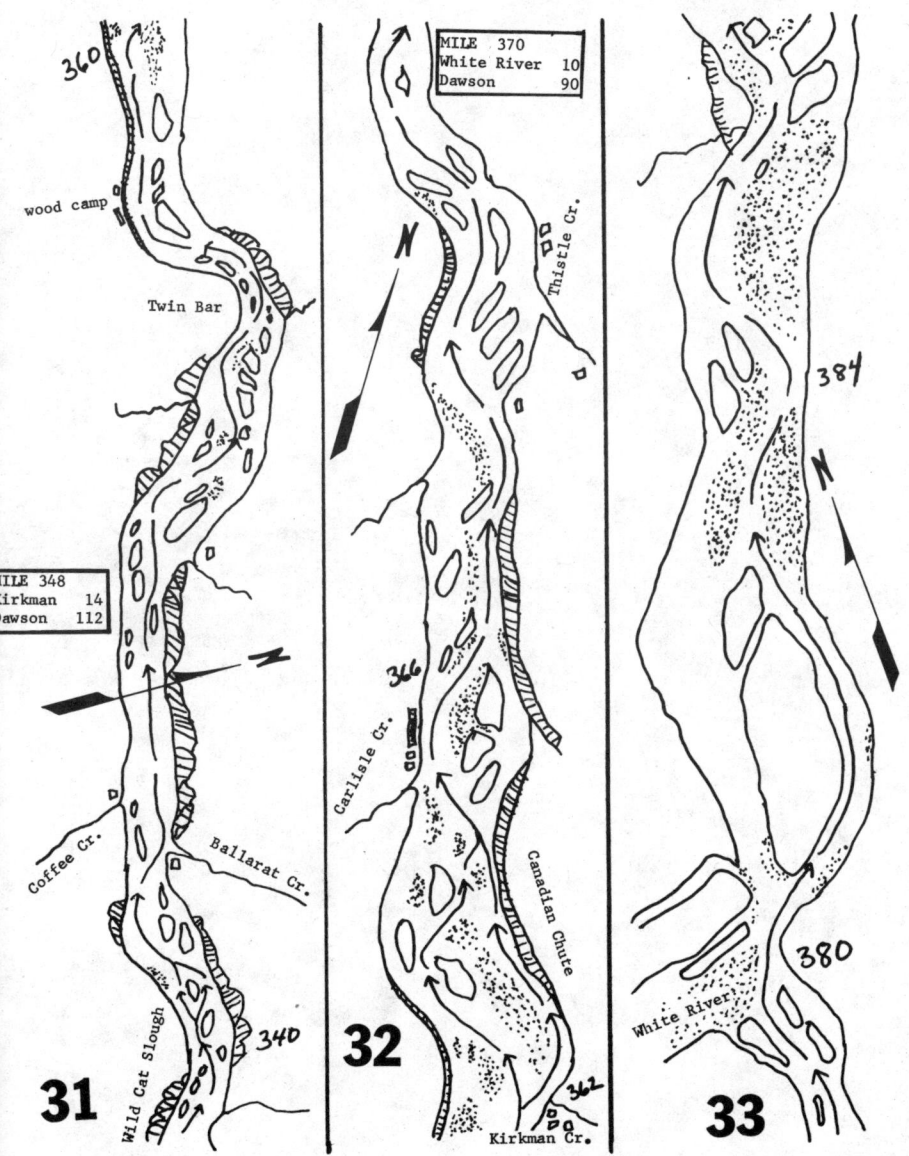

Thistle Creek roadhouse

Canyon topography below Stewart River

using privately-owned cabins if possible. There are many other adequate campsites.

One of the most interesting towns along this stretch is Thistle Creek, set far back in the woods from the river. It was an old roadhouse and steamboat stop, and a road leads back up the creek to a mine. Thistle Creek also is privately-owned and the owner is attempting to preserve it as a museum of the period. The two-story roadhouse still has furniture, books and other items that make it look like an unstaffed museum. A clearing down by the river, formerly a pasture, is a good campsite but also a great breeding ground for mosquitos. It is best to camp on one of the islands or exposed sandbars.

A few miles beyond Thistle Creek the river becomes grayer as the White River enters with its massive load of silt from the St. Elias Range. The big river adds considerably to the Yukon's load and it becomes more than a mile wide for most of the remainder of the trip. It is best to fill canteens and jugs with water from side streams from here to Dawson City, although many people do drink the river water after letting the dirt settle to the bottom.

Lanterns left behind at Thistle Creek

Fort Selkirk to Dawson City and Journey's End   123

Stewart Island

Ten miles from the White River's entrance is Stewart Island, at the mouth of the Stewart River. Rudi and Yvonne Burian have lived on the island most of their lives, and they operate a small store that has been in existence since the gold rush era. In addition to the store, they have built several small rental cabins with everything provided except bedding. The Burians are very knowledgable on the Yukon and its history, and a stop to visit with them should definitely be on the itinerary.

The island has been victimized by the Yukon, and nearly every spring the river carves off a big chunk of the island and washes it away.

The store has only a few items, such as refreshments and basic food needs, but a candy bar and bottle of cold pop can be a welcome duo after a few hot days on the river. Occasionally

Abandoned woodcutter's camp near Sixty Mile River mouth

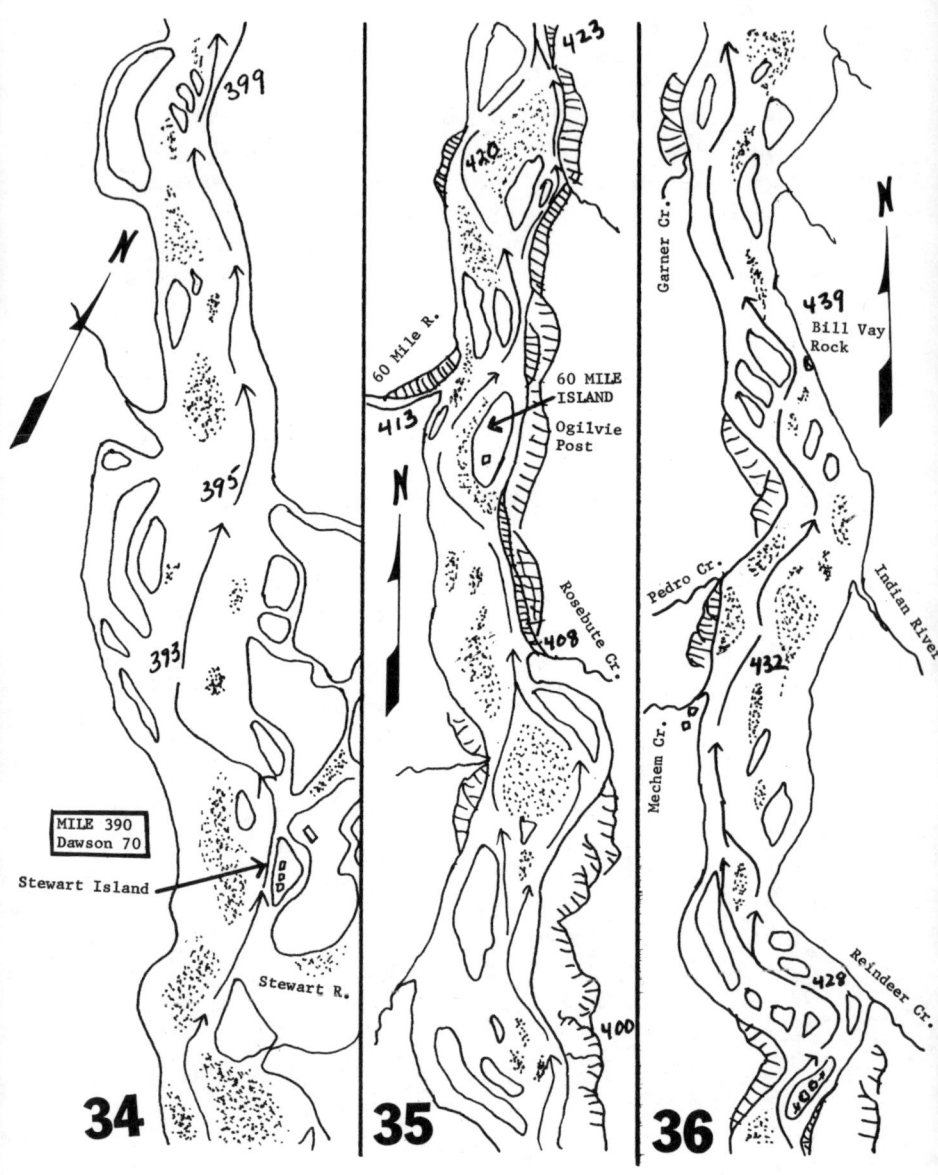

Front Street, Dawson City, in the summer of 1899

the Burians will have pelts for sale, such as ermine and fox, since they trap during the winter.

They also have a small museum near the store with artifacts they've picked up along the Stewart and Yukon, including a large selection of rare bottles. None are for sale, however.

A visit with the Burians also prepares you for your reentry into civilization. They live 70 miles from the nearest town (Dawson City), but they have a broad, grassy lawn they keep mowed neatly, and during nice weather they sit outside in lawn chairs and watch the river flow past. The Burians tend to dispel many of the images we have of the Yukon; of people living in cabins with dirt floors and of them being away from civilization so long they forget how to talk.

The Stewart River had a small gold rush on it that was overshadowed by the Klondike strike. However, Jack London wintered over on the Stewart in 1898-99, and things he saw and heard that winter resulted in many of his famous, if exaggerated, stories.

Later, Stewart Island was an important barge terminal when steamboats ran the Stewart delivering goods to the mine at Mayo and hauling ore downstream.

Last Overnight Camp

Numerous campsites with good supplies of firewood can be found almost at will along the river between Stewart Island and Dawson City. Some boaters have found it a boon to their morale to go up the Sixtymile River a short distance and camp the last night before entering Dawson City. The Sixtymile isn't as cold as the Yukon and you can bathe in it without undue discomfort.

Directly across from the mouth of the Sixtymile River is one of the river's more important historic spots. Variously called Sixtymile Island and Ogilvie Post, it was here the first post office in the Yukon was built. Joe LaDue, the trader who operated the post, was the founder of Dawson City when he abandoned Ogilvie Post and headed downstream to start a new town and, in the process, become a wealthy man operating a sawmill and selling off business lots. Several cabins remain in various stages of decay.

Grand Forks Junction of Eldorado and Bonanza Creek, which was a thriving town during the height of the gold mining.

New cabin near Stewart River

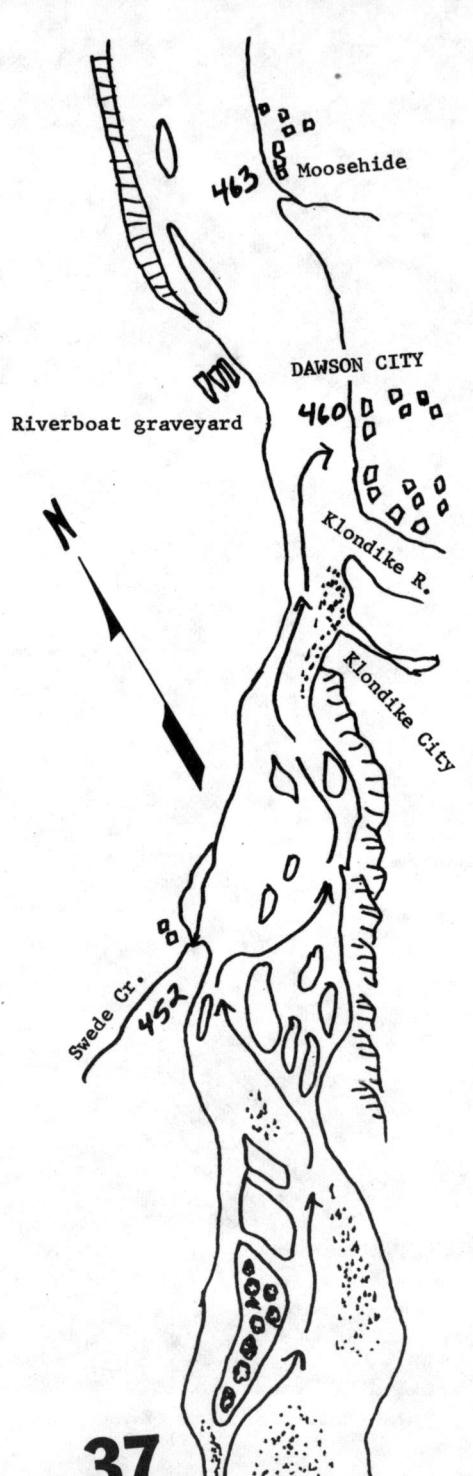

Moon over Yukon River just outside Dawson City

Dawson City from river with the distinctive slide scar above town.

Fort Selkirk to Dawson City and Journey's End 131

This is the last day on the river for most boaters and you know the trip is over when you see a bald spot on a mountainside ahead. That is the slide scar that marks Dawson City and has been a beacon for boaters on the river since the 1890s. The scar has been called Moosehide, and an Indian village three miles downstream has the same name. According to Indian oral history, the slide covered a village centuries ago, and according to Indian legends, a band of Indians from another tribe caused the slide to cover their enemy's campsite.

Old building in Dawson City canted by permafrost thawing

Bow shot of steamboat *Keno*, a museum at Dawson City

View of Dawson City, Yukon River and highway from Midnight Dome (Wayne Towriss, Government of the Yukon Tourism & Information Branch)

Dawson City

As you approach Dawson City, you will have to cut across the current of the Klondike River as it enters the Yukon, but it creates a backwater the steamboats used to get to shore. The best place to land is in the vicinity of the old paddlewheeler, *Keno*, now a museum on the bank. This is in the heart of town and you'll have a shorter distance to carry your gear from the river to hotels.

You will probably have to restrain yourself from bragging to locals that you just came down the river in a boat, all the way from headwaters. They won't be impressed because they've

The Vern Gorst claim at 16 Above Eldorado. Gorst made a fortune in the gold rush and founded Pacific Air Transport on the West Coast several years later, which was the parent company to United Air Lines.

done it numerous times, their parents did it and hundreds of people do it each year. Yukoners are difficult to impress. However, if you're bursting with enthusiasm and must talk to somebody, seek out a well-dressed tourist and tell him. Tourists are more easily impressed and want to meet someone as scruffy as yourself so they will have something else to talk about back home. Some will even insist on taking a picture of you. Don't smile. Look ominous.

Dawson City has been described by many writers as an eccentric little town. Perhaps individualistic would be a kinder word, because it is definitely not your usual small town. With its colorful history and its knack of attracting strong personalities for permanent residents, you sometimes will have the feeling you've stepped off the river onto a movie set.

Until the end of the steamboat era, Dawson City was the major city in the Yukon, and also was the territorial capital. The old Commissioner's Residence still stands in good repair at

Former bawdy house named Ruby's Place being restored by federal government.

Palace Grand Theater, left, and Post Office, both being restored.

the upriver edge of town, but the government was moved to Whitehorse in 1953, so the residence stands vacant. After the government left, the town's population dwindled and the vacated homes and cabins became targets for vandals.

During the past few years, Dawson City has become more and more like a live-in museum. The Canadian government has budgeted at least $10 million for restoration and preservation, and several of the old swaybacked buildings that might have soon fallen in on themselves have been jacked up and new foundations installed to avoid the uncertainties of building on permafrost. All new buildings in Dawson City now are built either on high pads of gravel or on steel pilings driven deep into the ground.

The town's showplace is the Palace Grand Theater, where performances of musical comedy and English music hall-type reviews are given during the summer months. The theater originally was built by Arizona Charlie Meadows during the Klondike heyday, burned, rebuilt and then allowed to fall into a state of disrepair after the population dwindled. In 1960 the Klondike Visitors Association bought it and turned it over to the federal government the following year for restoration to its 1899 appearance. The theater is open during the day for tours and photographs.

There is an automobile campground in town, but those tent camping should plan on going across the Yukon River to set up their tents. This avoids whatever problem with vandalism and theft may exist in town. A free ferry runs back and forth across the river and docks downstream a short distance from the *Keno*. There is a public shower service and laundromat at the Northwestern Motel.

Among the other attractions in town are Robert Service's cabin at Eighth and Church Streets, where readings of his poetry are given during the afternoons in summer; the "Gold Room" in the top floor of the Bank of Commerce on the river bank, where various measuring and weighing devices are exhibited; half of Jack London's cabin (the other half was hauled to Jack London Square in San Francisco); or simply strolling around town taking in the sights.

Some maps still show Klondike City, which locals call Louse-

Dawson City from a hill overlooking Klondike City (better known as Lousetown) in the foreground. Dawson City is in the background across the Klondike River.

A packtrain of gold from Eldorado Creek on its way to Dawson City didn't need armed guards; there was no place for a thief to go if he should rob it.

town, on the opposite side of the Klondike River. Nearly everything is gone now and it is hardly worth the effort to go over there. The settlement became the red-light district for Dawson City, and clients traveled back and forth on a rickety footbridge, which made if difficult for men to consort with the ladies over there without being seen by someone.

Since you have followed the "Trail of '98" to the Klondike, a visit to the goldfields should be considered part of the package. And it is much better to go on a guided tour than to rent a car and go out without benefit of a guide.

Today, about all that remains of the original stampede is the long, curving piles of dredge tailings left behind the Guggenheim-owned dredges that followed the first miners. Bonanza Creek, where the discovery was made, is reached by driving along a road built atop the dredge tailings, and you pass the dredge that did the damage, a huge, four-story monster that cranked and groaned and whistled while turning out a pitifully small-looking stream of gold. Old-timers say that watching one of the dredges work was like watching a carnival; they were so huge, so noisy, yet went to all that work to turn out something measured in ounces rather than tons.

If you should arrive in Dawson City toward the longest day of the year—June 22—you will want to join the stampede to the top of Midnight Dome overlooking Dawson City and the river. It is a tradition that most Dawsonites observe and big parties are sometimes held up there. Back in town, a baseball game starts at midnight each year with no playing field lights necessary.

A good hike from Dawson City can be made along the face of the slide scar and down a trail to Moosehide, the abandoned Indian village. A tour boat runs the same route several times a day, but most people who have spent two weeks in a boat prefer walking. The trail climbs to the top of the high cliffs overlooking the river, then drops back down again to the wide valley occupied by Moosehide. The town was originally where most Indians in the area lived, but over the years they moved into Dawson City for mining and service industry jobs, and eventually abandoned the town entirely.

The Anglican church had a mission there with a church, school and teachers' quarters. Most of the church furniture is still intact, including a pump organ that works and hymn books. The school building still has the desks and some furniture, and the teachers' quarters upstairs appear almost ready to move into.

You can make arrangements with the tour boat operator to ride down to the village and walk back, or vice versa.

The Nugget Express was a mail and grocery service established during the gold rush, which later failed.

An open air store in Dawson City, summer of 1898

Modern mining on Bonanza Creek with bulldozer, water pump and sluice box

Tourists panning for gold on Bonanza Creek

Abandoned Dredge No. 4 on Bonanza Creek

Abandoned dredge on Hunker Creek

Dredge tailings along Klondike River with highway at right rear

Old shipyard with wrecked *Julia B.*, *Seattle* and *Schwatka* just downstream from Dawson City.

View upstream to Dawson City from Moosehide, three miles from Dawson City

7

Tributary Rivers

Many canoeists or kayakers prefer avoiding the busy Yukon River and lake system by taking trips down the tributary streams that join the Yukon between Lake Laberge and Dawson City. The major navigable rivers are the Teslin, Big Salmon, Pelly, Macmillan, White, Stewart and Sixty Mile (or Sixtymile) Rivers.

Brief summaries of those rivers which follow are taken from a series of wild river surveys made in 1971 by four-man canoe teams sponsored by the Department of Indian Affairs and Northern Development, National and Historic Parks Branch. Leader of the survey was Ian Donaldson, who wrote the reports and made them available to the public. Copies are available through the Travel and Information Branch, Yukon Territorial Government, Box 2703, Whitehorse, Y.T.

An unidentified tributary stream.

Since these rivers are more remote and less traveled than the Yukon and the lake system, it cannot be overemphasized that only experienced canoeists or kayakers should attempt them, and that safety precautions should be taken at all times.

The author has not traveled on these rivers, but he can verify the accuracy and conclusions of Donaldson's reports on the lakes and Yukon River.

Teslin River

ACCESS: You can enter the water at either the town of Teslin (Mile 804 on the Alaska Highway) on Lake Teslin, or Johnson's Crossing (Mile 837) on the Teslin River to bypass the lake.

MILEAGE: Donaldson's crew traveled the 260 miles from Teslin to Carmacks in 13 days.

HISTORICAL SIGNIFICANCE: This route was used by some gold rushers who came up the Inside Passage to Wrangell, Alaska, then up the Stikine River to Telegraph Creek, B.C., then overland to Teslin Lake. A steamboat service operated three years on the lake and river, which resulted in formation of Teslin, Johnson's Crossing, McClintock, Teslin Crossing, Mason Landing and Hootalinqua, all of which are ghost towns today.

A telegraph line was built between Telegraph Creek and Hootalinqua, where it linked to the wire down the Yukon River and back over White Pass to Skagway.

NAVIGATION: The Teslin presents no difficulty for experienced boaters. There are a few sets of rapids, particularly in the Boswell Creek area and Roaring Bull Rapids, but they are not rated as dangerous. It is recommended, however, that all rapids be scouted on foot before entering.

Big Salmon River

ACCESS: Quiet Lake on the Canol Road, Mile 46 (from Johnson's Crossing).

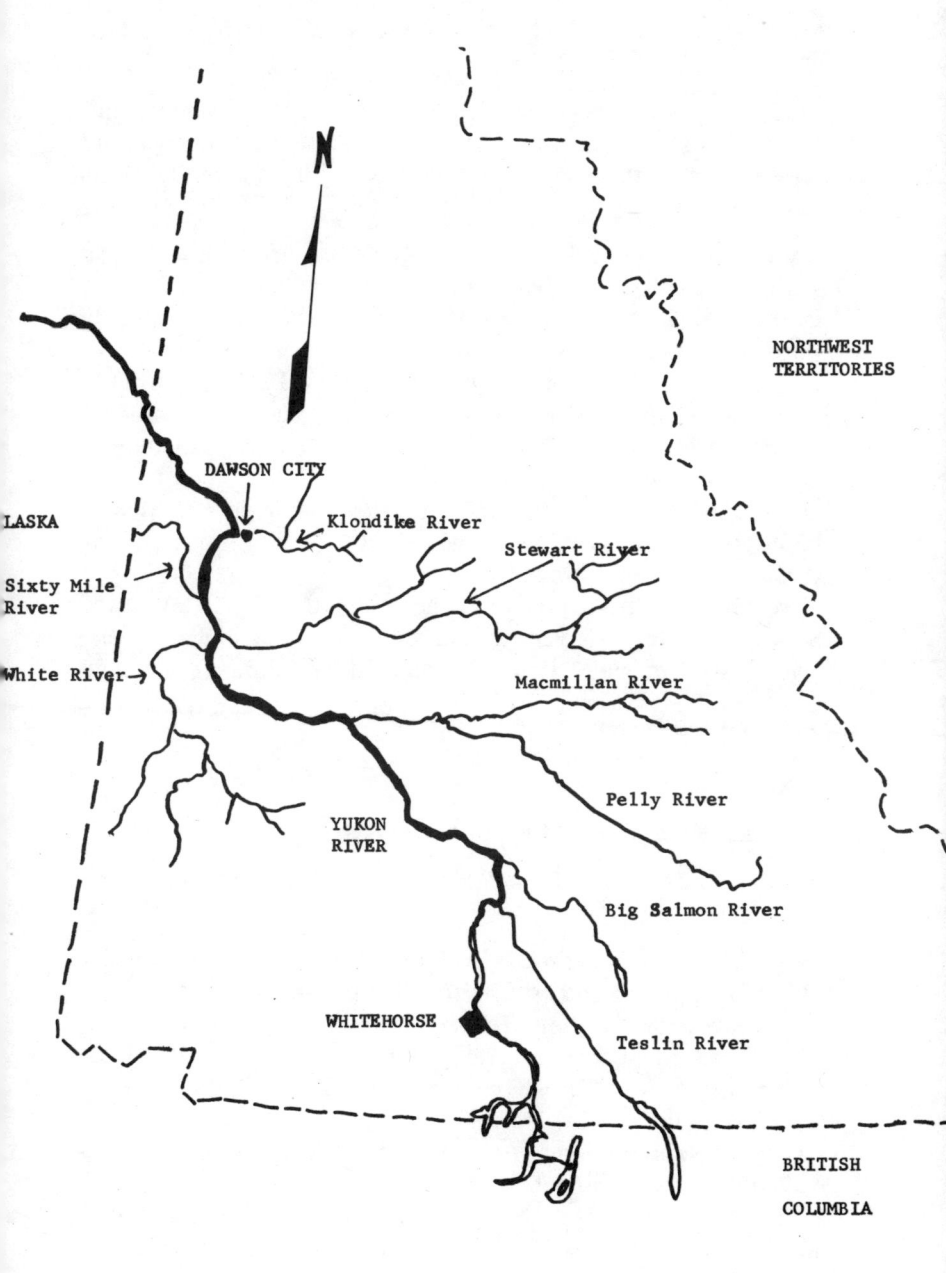

MILEAGE: Approximately 247 miles from the south end of Quiet Lake to Carmacks in 10 days.

RIVER CHARACTERISTICS: Little historical significance, but noted for its wilderness character. No pollution in the river and no man-made structures are found until the Yukon River is reached.

NAVIGATION: Quiet Lake is connected to Sandy Lake by a shallow, swift stream that is bordered by willows which make landings difficult. The banks of the Big Salmon are frequently lined with sweepers which constitute a hazard. Other banks range upward to 75 feet high, also making landings difficult. There are numerous rapids on the river varying from one-hundred feet to more than a thousand feet long. Fortunately, it is possible to pull out for scouting before entering most rapids. Some may present problems during low-water periods due to boulders and bars. Portaging would involve brush-beating through dense undergrowth.

A whirlpool occurs at the junction of the Big Salmon and South Big Salmon Rivers with a vortex about a foot deep and five to six feet wide. It can be avoided by following the right limit of the Big Salmon.

Pelly River

ACCESS: Ross River, Mile 138, Canol Road.

MILEAGE: 249 miles from Ross River to Fort Selkirk, Yukon River; eight days.

HISTORICAL SIGNIFICANCE: Robert Campbell, the Hudson's Bay Co. explorer and trader, traveled down the Pelly in 1840 and founded Fort Pelly Banks at the junction of Campbell Creek and the Pelly, and later Fort Selkirk where the Pelly enters the Yukon. In 1898 George M. Dawson followed the same route for the Geological Survey of Canada and wrote one of the most literate reports ever composed on what then was called the Yukon district.

Today the river is still largely untouched by civilization outside the towns of Ross River and Pelly Crossing. You have the

Tributary Rivers

choice of leaving the river at Pelly Crossing on the Dawson Highway, or continuing on to Fort Selkirk and down the river to Dawson City.

NAVIGATION: There are three sets of rapids between the Faro Bridge and Pelly Crossing which the skilled canoeist will find no difficulty navigating: Little and Big Fishhook Rapids and those in Granite Canyon. They may pose problems during periods of high water, and should definitely be scouted. Both Big and Little Fishhook Rapids are rated Grade I difficulty at low water and Grade II at high water. Granite Canyon is rated Grade I at the entrance and more difficult farther into the canyon, again depending on the water level. The easiest course is along the right limit, and scouting is required.

Donaldson broke the trip down into three stages in his report:

Ross River to Faro—43 miles, two days' travel, no rapids.

Faro to Pelly Crossing—163 miles, two days, Grade II rapids.

Pelly Crossing to Fort Selkirk—43 miles, two days, no rapids.

Macmillan River

ACCESS: This is the most remote of the Yukon tributaries, and access is either up the unimproved Canol Road with four-wheel drive vehicles or by charter aircraft. The Canol crosses the upper river approximately 60 miles beyond Ross River.

MILEAGE: Donaldson's crew entered the river at Russell Creek some miles below the Canol Highway and traveled 145 miles to the mouth of the river where it empties into the Pelly.

RIVER CHARACTERISTICS: It is the most remote and one of the most beautiful rivers in the Yukon Territory. Surrounded by mountains and dense forests, it also has one of the highest wildlife populations.

NAVIGATION: There are no major rapids on the river, with the major difficulties being log jams and sweepers, both of which are easy to avoid. The overall rating of the river is Grade I, although those entering the river from the Canol Road are encouraged to seek information locally since Donaldson did not survey it.

White River

ACCESS: This is the least interesting river of all those surveyed, one generally described as not worth the effort. It is heavily laden with silt from the St. Elias Range and flows through generally uninteresting topography. However, for those who insist, it is accessible from the town of Snag, 17 miles off the Alaska Highway at Mile 1188.

MILEAGE: Eight days for the 180 miles to Dawson City (the White enters the Yukon 80 miles from Dawson City).

RIVER CHARACTERISTICS: It is one of the major tributaries of the Yukon and was used as a main route from the Yukon to the Chisana gold rush in Alaska in 1913. A pack train service operated between Coffee Creek and Chisana for a short time. The milky river is characterized by swift (average is 5 miles per hour) water, often choppy, with back eddies and frequent sweepers and log jams. The water is not potable due to the high silt content, and side streams should be used for water. As if the other undesirable characteristics were not enough, the river banks have a number of discarded oil drums and other debris.

Stewart River

ACCESS: The access from a road is at Mayo, although Donaldson went by plane to the headwaters at Beaver Creek.

MILEAGE: Two weeks to Dawson City which includes one day from Stewart Island to Dawson City.

RIVER CHARACTERISTICS: The roughest part of the river is between Beaver Creek and the town of Mayo, and those interested in chartering a plane to that area should obtain a copy of Donaldson's report. For the purposes of this book, the description will be limited to that part of the river easily accessible by highway. Suffice it to say that the upper river involves

Tributary Rivers

portaging around waterfalls and especially rough sets of rapids, and should not be attempted by novices.

Below Mayo the river is not potable and the highway follows it closely until just below Stewart Crossing on the main highway. The stretch along here is the least interesting of the entire river, and most canoeists will prefer putting into the water at Stewart Crossing and continuing down to the Yukon River. Below the crossing, the valley narrows for a few miles, then widens again with islands and sloughs being formed. A few cabins can be seen and evidence of the major gold rush there in the 1890s. Most are protected by the territorial government, including the Maisy May Ranch that was used as a hay ranch to supply the horse-powered winter road between Dawson City and Whitehorse.

Sixtymile River

ACCESS: The river is reached by turning off the so-called "Top of the World" Highway that connects Dawson City to the Alaska Highway. The turnoff is 55 miles west of Dawson City, and 20 miles west of the Swede Dome turnoff. The turnoff road leads to the abandoned settlement of Sixtymile on Glacier Creek. A four-wheel drive vehicle is needed to navigate the road.

MILEAGE: Donaldson's crew took five days to run the Sixtymile to its mouth, plus an additional day to paddle downstream 50 miles to Dawson City.

RIVER CHARACTERISTICS: The overall rating of the river is Grade II with frequent but easily navigable rapids during low-water periods. During heavy runoff, the difficulty would increase. During the low-water periods of late summer (August), a sturdy canoe is required because the river is so shallow that the bottom would be scraped frequently. Lining, hauling and portaging are often necessary and good footgear should be worn. The river water is potable.

Suggested Reading

Atlin Centennial Committee, *Atlin 1898-1910*, available from the committee at Atlin and some northern bookstores. $2. A history of the area, well-researched and informative.

Berton, Pierre, *Klondike*, McClelland & Stewart, Toronto. Revised 1973. $10. The definitive history of the gold rush. Not available in U.S. stores at this writing. Previously published in U.S. as *Klondike Fever*.

Berton, Pierre, *Drifting Home*, Knopf (U.S.) 1973. $6.95. An account of the Berton family's float trip down the Yukon River with flashbacks to his father's experiences in the gold rush and Dawson City.

Cantin, Eugene, *Yukon Summer*, Chronicle Publishing, San Francisco, 1973. $6.95. Account of Cantin's trip down the Yukon in a kayak.

Suggested Reading

Hunt, William R., *North of 53*, Macmillan. 1975. $12.95. Excellent account of smaller gold rushes and off-beat facts about the Klondike stampede.

Mathews, Richard, *The Yukon*, Holt, Rinehart & Winston. 1968. $7.50. One of the "Rivers of America" series, well written with most of the emphasis on the Alaskan Yukon.

Morgan, Murray, *One Man's Gold Rush*, U. of Washington Press. Seattle, 1967. $4.95 softcover. The famous E.A. Hegg photo collection that shows the gold rush and the Nome stampede, plus the building of the White Pass & Yukon Route.

Satterfield, Archie, *Chilkoot Pass*, Alaska Northwest Publishing, Edmonds, Wash., 1973. Revised 1974. $3.95. A history of Chilkoot Pass during the gold rush with a guide and maps to the present trail. Illustrated.

Wharton, David B., *The Alaska Gold Rush*, University of Indiana Press. 1972. $8.95. One of the best books to put the entire sequence of gold rushes in Alaska and the Yukon into their proper perspective.